Edgar Allan Poe

These and other titles are included in The Importance Of biography series:

Maya Angelou
Louis Armstrong
James Baldwin
The Beatles
Alexander Graham Bell
Napoleon Bonaparte
Julius Caesar
Rachel Carson
Charlie Chaplin
Charlemagne
Winston Churchill
Christopher Columbus
Leonardo da Vinci
James Dean
Charles Dickens
Walt Disney
Dr. Seuss
F. Scott Fitzgerald
Anne Frank
Benjamin Franklin
Mohandas Gandhi
John Glenn
Jane Goodall
Martha Graham

Lorraine Hansberry
Ernest Hemingway
Adolf Hitler
Harry Houdini
Thomas Jefferson
John F. Kennedy
Martin Luther King Jr.
Douglas MacArthur
Margaret Mead
Golda Meir
Mother Teresa
John Muir
Richard M. Nixon
Pablo Picasso
Elvis Presley
Queen Elizabeth I
Margaret Sanger
Oskar Schindler
William Shakespeare
Frank Sinatra
Tecumseh
Simon Wiesenthal

Edgar Allan Poe

by Rafael Tilton

Lucent Books, P.O. Box 289011, San Diego, CA 92198-9011

On Cover: Crayon portrait of Edgar Allan Poe by Flavius Fisher.

Library of Congress Cataloging-in-Publication Data

Tilton, Rafael.
    Edgar Allan Poe / by Rafael Tilton.
        p. cm.—(The importance of)
Includes bibliographical references (p.) and index.
    Summary: Profiles the life and work of Edgar Allan Poe, his classical education, his roles as author, journalist, and family man, and his financial problems and personal tragedies.
    ISBN 1-56006-845-0 (hardback : alk. paper)
    1. Poe, Edgar Allan, 1809–1849—Juvenile literature.
2. Authors, American—19th century—Biography—Juvenile literature. 3. Journalists—United States—Biography—Juvenile literature. [1. Poe, Edgar Allan, 1809–1849. 2. Authors, American.]
I. Title. II. Series.
    PS2631 .T55 2001
    818'.309—dc21

                                                2001000850

Contents

Foreword

THE IMPORTANCE OF biography series deals with individuals who have made a unique contribution to history. The editors of the series have deliberately chosen to cast a wide net and include people from all fields of endeavor. Individuals from politics, music, art, literature, philosophy, science, sports, and religion are all represented. In addition, the editors did not restrict the series to individuals whose accomplishments have helped change the course of history. Of necessity, this criterion would have eliminated many whose contribution was great, though limited. Charles Darwin, for example, was responsible for radically altering the scientific view of the natural history of the world. His achievements continue to impact the study of science today. Others, such as Chief Joseph of the Nez Percé, played a pivotal role in the history of their own people. While Joseph's influence does not extend much beyond the Nez Percé, his nonviolent resistance to white expansion and his continuing role in protecting his tribe and his homeland remain an inspiration to all.

These biographies are more than factual chronicles. Each volume attempts to emphasize an individual's contributions both in his or her own time and for posterity. For example, the voyages of Christopher Columbus opened the way to European colonization of the New World. Unquestionably, his encounter with the New World brought monumental changes to both Europe and the Americas in his day. Today, however, the broader impact of Columbus's voyages is being critically scrutinized. *Christopher Columbus,* as well as every biography in The Importance Of series, includes and evaluates the most recent scholarship available on each subject.

Each author includes a wide variety of primary and secondary source quotations to document and substantiate his or her work. All quotes are footnoted to show readers exactly how and where biographers derive their information, as well as provide stepping stones to further research. These quotations enliven the text by giving readers eyewitness views of the life and times of each individual covered in The Importance Of series.

Finally, each volume is enhanced by photographs, bibliographies, chronologies, and comprehensive indexes. For both the casual reader and the student engaged in research, The Importance Of biographies will be a fascinating adventure into the lives of people who have helped shape humanity's past and present, and who will continue to shape its future.

IMPORTANT DATES IN THE LIFE OF EDGAR ALLAN POE

1809
Edgar Poe born in Boston, Massachusetts, on January 19.

1819
Returns to Richmond, attends school with Thomas E. Clarke.

1830
Admitted to West Point in June.

1811
Poe's mother dies in Richmond, Virginia, on December 8. Poe is taken into the home of John and Frances Allan.

1826
Secretly engaged to Sarah Elmira Royster; attends University of Virginia from February to December.

1810 **1815** **1820** **1825** **1830**

1812
Christened Edgar Allan Poe but not adopted.

1827
Leaves Allan home on March 19; publishes *Tamerlane and Other Poems* anonymously in Boston; joins army on May 26.

1815
Sails with Allan family to London on June 23, attends school with the Misses Dubourg.

1829
Permitted to leave army on April 15 to apply for West Point; publishes *Al Aaraaf, Tamerlane and Minor Poems,* signed.

1831
Released from West Point on February 18; publishes *Poems.*

1818
Transfers to school with Reverend John Bransby near London.

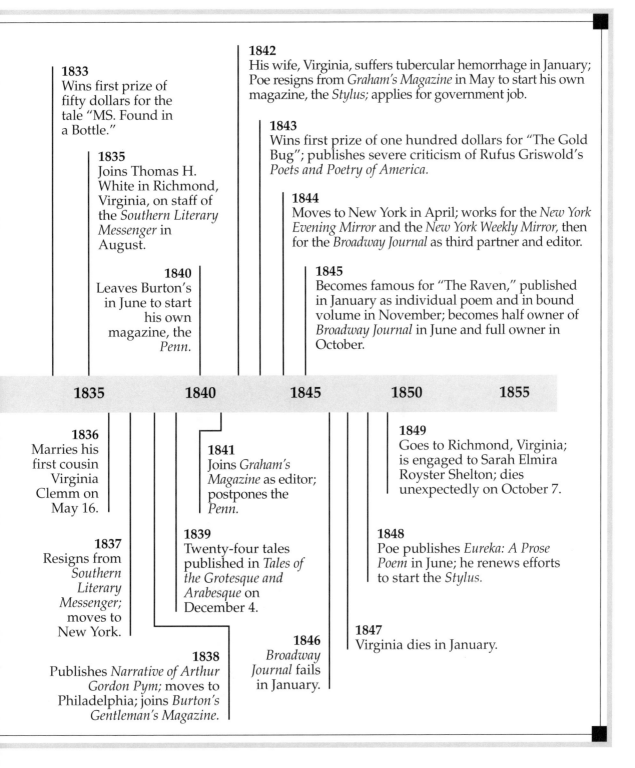

1833
Wins first prize of fifty dollars for the tale "MS. Found in a Bottle."

1835
Joins Thomas H. White in Richmond, Virginia, on staff of the *Southern Literary Messenger* in August.

1840
Leaves Burton's in June to start his own magazine, the *Penn.*

1842
His wife, Virginia, suffers tubercular hemorrhage in January; Poe resigns from *Graham's Magazine* in May to start his own magazine, the *Stylus;* applies for government job.

1843
Wins first prize of one hundred dollars for "The Gold Bug"; publishes severe criticism of Rufus Griswold's *Poets and Poetry of America.*

1844
Moves to New York in April; works for the *New York Evening Mirror* and the *New York Weekly Mirror,* then for the *Broadway Journal* as third partner and editor.

1845
Becomes famous for "The Raven," published in January as individual poem and in bound volume in November; becomes half owner of *Broadway Journal* in June and full owner in October.

| 1835 | 1840 | 1845 | 1850 | 1855 |

1836
Marries his first cousin Virginia Clemm on May 16.

1837
Resigns from *Southern Literary Messenger;* moves to New York.

1838
Publishes *Narrative of Arthur Gordon Pym;* moves to Philadelphia; joins *Burton's Gentleman's Magazine.*

1841
Joins *Graham's Magazine* as editor; postpones the *Penn.*

1839
Twenty-four tales published in *Tales of the Grotesque and Arabesque* on December 4.

1846
Broadway Journal fails in January.

1849
Goes to Richmond, Virginia; is engaged to Sarah Elmira Royster Shelton; dies unexpectedly on October 7.

1848
Poe publishes *Eureka: A Prose Poem* in June; he renews efforts to start the *Stylus.*

1847
Virginia dies in January.

Against the Current

The importance of Edgar Allan Poe to American literature is uncontested. For example, with the writing of his tale, "The Murders in the Rue Morgue," Poe is considered by many scholars to have invented the modern detective story. Others see in his incorporation of natural phenomena into such tales as "The Premature Burial" the beginnings of science fiction. Poe's poetry is widely considered to represent a major departure from the romantic works of poets such as William Cullen Bryant and to have influenced the work of others, such as Walt Whitman.

In almost every kind of writing Poe did, he went against what was at the time ac-

American writer Edgar Allan Poe was both innovative and prolific and his powerful works are still popular today.

cepted practice. At a time when American poets were producing lengthy epics such as Henry Wadsworth Longfellow's *Hiawatha*, Poe was writing poems that in relatively few words both created a distinct mood and told a story. In his book reviews he refused to praise poor writing even when struggling publishers would have preferred that he do so.

Above all else, Poe valued artistic excellence. In writing poetry, he followed the principle that creating works of beauty superseded the conveying of moral messages. Thanks to his skilled control of language and style in poems that were aesthetically pleasing, Poe's work continues to be enjoyed by readers, while that of many of his contemporaries has fallen into obscurity.

In his personal life, Poe defied his contemporaries' opinion that the public respect paid to a writer should depend upon his or her behavior. Instead, Poe believed that one's literary reputation should be based on the unity and truth of one's works. Although Poe was severely criticized by other writers of his day for what they perceived as his violation of standards of personal behavior, time has vindicated Poe's conviction that his works would be his real legacy.

Adding poignancy to Poe's story is the fact that he produced a prolific variety of essays, tales, and poems despite the low pay accorded to writers during this time in U.S. history. Poe's desperate poverty and the personal tragedy that accompanied it added power to his works even as they cut short his life and the lives of those he loved.

Poe's rise to popularity by the time he was thirty-five resulted from the fortuitous combination of genius, temperament, and the public's literary taste at the time. Drawn to the literary arts from his early years, he was able to make uncannily good use of his imagination, his reading, and his analytical powers to produce original and powerful tales, essays, and poems that would long outlast their creator.

1 A Classical Education

Edgar Poe was born on January 19, 1809, in Boston, Massachusetts, to a pair of itinerant actors, David Poe Jr. and Elizabeth Poe. The troupe for which the Poes worked was fulfilling an extended engagement in Boston at the time of Edgar's birth.

The Poe family name was already well regarded by the time Edgar was born. Edgar's grandparents had come from Ireland and settled in eastern Pennsylvania in the middle of the eighteenth century. His grandfather, David Poe Sr., was an American patriot who had moved to Baltimore, Maryland, where he became quartermaster general for the Continental army during the Revolutionary War. Edgar's grandmother, Elizabeth Cairnes Poe, also had joined the colonists' war effort by making clothes for the Baltimore militiamen who were fighting for American independence.

David Poe Jr. had been encouraged by his parents to become a lawyer, but he wanted to become an actor. So against his parents' wishes, Poe joined a touring theater company and by 1803 was acting in Charleston, South Carolina. The younger Poe was not destined to succeed as an actor, however. Although reviewers noted his clear and melodious voice, they also pointed to his lack of acting ability. Poe persisted for a

time, however, and in the course of his pursuit of jobs on stage, he eventually met the recently widowed Elizabeth Arnold Hopkins. They married in January 1806, a union that the Poe family did not approve.

Unlike her husband, nineteen-year-old Elizabeth was an accomplished actress who had spent nearly her entire life on the stage. At the time she married Poe, she had been receiving favorable reviews for her performances for over fifteen years. Elizabeth was especially well liked in Boston. In roles such as that of Cordelia in Shakespeare's *King Lear*, she was enthusiastically applauded by her audiences.

The Poes continued their respective acting careers as they started their family. Their first son, William Henry Leonard Poe, was born in Boston in 1807. In spite of Elizabeth's popularity, however, the acting couple's income as players in a traveling troupe was inadequate to allow them to raise a child, so David's parents in Baltimore soon took over the care of the little boy.

A Mysterious Disappearance

Edgar was born two years after his brother. This time, the Poes kept their child with them, but the family was not destined to be together for long. Before the end of Edgar's first year, his father disappeared without a trace. Whether he died and his body was found but not identified, or whether Poe simply deserted his family and lived out his life in anonymity, remains a mystery.

Poe's disappearance left the family in desperate poverty. Elizabeth, who at the time of her husband's disappearance was expecting her third child, continued her acting career, and in July 1810, she took Edgar with her as the company moved south on tour. Elizabeth Poe's mother, also an actress, was in the same troupe and shared living quarters with her daughter and grandson. But theater performers earned money only

Despite Elizabeth Poe's success as an actress, her income was not enough to support her family.

when they were acting, so with the birth of Rosalie Poe in December, the family's income dropped yet again.

Soon after Rosalie's birth, Elizabeth, her mother, and two youngest children rejoined the troupe, which had moved on to Richmond, Virginia. Elizabeth's skills as an actress must have been undiminished by childbearing, for a *Richmond Enquirer* review of *The Belle's Stratagem* contained this complimentary comment about her acting:

> From an actress who possesses so eminently the faculty of pleasing, whose powers are so general and whose exertions are so ready, it would be unjust to withhold the tribute of applause. Were I to say simply that she is a valuable acquisition to the Theatre, I should dishonor her merit and do injustice to the feelings of the public. . . . Her "exits and her entrances" equally operate their electric effects, for if we expect to be pleased when Mrs. Poe appears, when her part is ended, our admiration ever proclaims that our anticipations have been more than realized.[1]

Elizabeth Poe continued to be successful in Richmond throughout the next several months. But in spite of her success with the audiences, Elizabeth's income was inadequate to support her family. Worse, she was clearly suffering the effects of a disease that was especially common among the poor in the early nineteenth century—tuberculosis. By October 11, 1811, her last performance, the situation was extreme, says Poe biographer Vincent Buranelli, and Elizabeth was "struggling desperately to survive, failing

MEDICINE ADMINISTERED IN GOOD FAITH

Shortly before the death in Richmond, Virginia, of Poe's actress mother, Elizabeth Arnold Poe, she and her children Edgar and Rosalie were visited by the woman who later became Rosalie's godmother, Jane Scott Mackenzie. Her later description of child-rearing practices she observed and disapproved of is included in The Home Life of Edgar Allan Poe, *by Mrs. Susan Weiss, and quoted in* The Poe Log, *edited by Dwight Thomas and David K. Jackson.*

"On occasion of her [Jane Scott Mackenzie's] first visit to the Poes, she had observed that the children were thin and pale and very fretful. To quiet them, their old nurse—whom Mrs. Poe in her last days addressed as 'Mother,' . . . took them upon her lap and fed them liberally with bread soaked in gin, when they soon fell asleep. Subsequently, after the death of the parents, the old woman (who remained in Richmond until her death, not long after, devoting herself to the children) acknowledged to Mrs. Mackenzie that she had, from the very birth of the girl [Rosalie] freely administered to them gin and other spirituous liquors, with sometimes laudanum [a drinkable form of opium], 'to make them strong and healthy,' or to put them to sleep when restless. Mrs. Mackenzie was convinced that this woman, who was a simple, honest creature, was, in reality, the maternal grandmother of the children, and conscientiously acted for their good."

with frightening rapidity until her earthly sorrows were finally stilled."[2]

A NEW LIFE FOR EDGAR

Throughout Elizabeth's illness, a number of charitable women from Richmond had showed an interest in her and her children. After Elizabeth died on December 8, 1811, these women gave her a Christian burial. One of the ladies, Frances Keeling Valentine Allan, took over the care of Edgar, who

was not quite three years old, while Mrs. William Mackenzie, her close friend and neighbor, took Rosalie.

Edgar settled into a somewhat ambiguous relationship with the Allans. John Allan, the man who became his foster father, was a Scottish-American tobacco merchant who had a hardheaded attitude about earning and spending money. He allowed the child to receive the name Edgar Allan Poe in a formal christening ceremony in 1812. He did not, however, adopt him, although a letter from Edgar's aunt Eliza Poe referred to the Allans as Edgar's "adopted parents."[3] At the same time that he treated Edgar well, Allan was somewhat reserved in his affection. Moreover, Allan had other calls on both his affection and his finances. Unbeknownst to his wife, John was keeping a mistress, by whom he had a son named Edwin Collier, who was a year or two older than Edgar.

Edgar's relationship with his foster mother was a great deal warmer. Frances Allan, because she had no children of her own, was particularly devoted to him. So was her sister, Nancy Valentine, who also lived with the Allans. The two women pampered him, dressed him in fancy clothes, and made as much of the precocious and appealing child as if he were their own son.

During his first years with the Allans, Edgar's life was one of privilege. The slaves who were part of the Allan household saw to his daily needs. When he was five, he joined children of other well-off Richmond families in school, where he studied spelling and arithmetic and was

Poe's foster father, John Allan, was a tobacco merchant.

tutored in the manners and attitudes of Southern society.

Despite the comforts Edgar and his foster family enjoyed, John Allan's affluence was something of an illusion. Allan's business relied on transatlantic trade, and that trade had been nearly cut off for years by ongoing warfare between England and France. Even neutral countries found their trade with the combatants hampered. Once America had sided with France in this conflict and then declared war on England in 1812, the situation had worsened.

For a time, John Allan was able to shelter his family from the effects of his declining finances, but even after the war between England and the United States ended in 1814, trade did not resume with its previous vigor. In hopes of reopening and expanding foreign markets for his tobacco, John Allan sailed for London on June 23, 1815.

Allan took his family along for what he expected would be an extended stay abroad. Six-year-old Edgar apparently thrived during the voyage. In a letter to his business partner, Charles Ellis, John Allan wrote: "Edgar says Pa say something for me, say I was not afraid coming across the Sea."[4]

After arriving in England, the Allans undertook a journey through Scotland. There, John Allan visited with members of his family. In places like Kilmarnock, Irvine, and Glasgow, little Edgar met vari-

Poe's first stay in Richmond, Virginia (pictured), ended when he was just six years old, when he and the Allan family moved to London, England.

ous cousins and other relations of his foster parents. Galts, Allans, and Fowlds, all were in some way related to John and Frances Allan.

Frances Allan, however, was unwell. Like Edgar's own mother, Frances was suffering from tuberculosis. As was common practice among the well-to-do, Frances sought treatment at a mineral bath. Edgar, meanwhile, was enrolled at a school in the London suburb of Chelsea, and rather than staying at the Allans' rented apartment, he lived with his two teachers, the Misses Dubourg.

A CLASSICAL EDUCATION

Edgar attended the Dubourgs' school for just over a year. After that his schooling was entrusted to the Reverend John Bransby at the Manor House School, located in the town of Stoke Newington, about four miles from London. Here Edgar learned to like reading and poetry, studied mathematics, French, and Latin, and perfected his knowledge of English grammar. His progress clearly pleased John Allan, who noted in a letter to his uncle William Galt that "Edgar is growing wonderfully and enjoys a good reputation as both able and willing to receive instruction."[5]

His foster father's approval of Edgar's achievement in Latin, French, and mathematics seemed, however, to mean little to the youngster, who was unhappy at school. Years later, Edgar Allan Poe would say of his schooling, "Since the sad experience of my schoolboy days to this present writing, I have seen little to sustain the notion held by

The Poe Family in Great Britain 1815

North Sea

North Atlantic Ocean

SCOTLAND

The Poes Tour Scotland

Glasgow

North Channel

Kilmarnock

Irvine

Irish Sea

Edgar Attends School Near London

IRELAND

ENGLAND

WALES

London

Strait of Dover

English Channel FRANCE

some folks, that schoolboys are the happiest of all mortals."[6]

AN END OF PROSPERITY

Edgar's school success in England might have destined him to go on to attend one of the great British universities such as Oxford or Cambridge, but five years in London failed to bring John Allan the hoped-for upswing in his business, and in 1819 he decided to return to America. With his business failing, Allan's finances were so meager that he was barely able to scrape together enough cash to pay for the family's passage back to Richmond, Virginia.

Once the family was back in America, the financial pressures eased somewhat. Thanks to a mortgage against their home, the Allans had the cash to live comfortably. Over the next few years, they continued to provide Edgar with the same education enjoyed by the children of the other upper-class families of Richmond. As he had in England, Edgar did well in his studies. He excelled in Latin and theater. He also wrote some poetry that impressed the headmaster, Joseph E. Clarke, and even his own family. In fact, writes biographer Jeffrey Meyers, "when Poe was eleven years old, his foster father, John Allan, showed Clarke a manuscript volume of his poems, which the ambitious boy wanted to have published. But Clarke, thinking this would flatter Poe's inordinate vanity, advised against publication and the project was dropped."[7]

Still, academic success did not translate into popularity with Edgar's classmates. Writing poetry made Edgar different from his American classmates, and his attitude toward the other students also set him apart. Poe biographer Hervey Allen writes, "The young Poe . . . seems to have been a precocious and somewhat lordly young gentleman."[8]

In addition to projecting an air of superiority, Edgar often acted as though he expected his classmates to defer to his wishes. As one biographer later noted, he could occasionally display generosity, but nobody considered him kind or even particularly friendly.

Despite Edgar's superior and perhaps melancholy attitude, a few boys followed his leadership—to their own detriment. For example, the son of Allan's partner, T. H. Ellis, later said he got into a lot of trouble on account of Edgar, who "led me to do many a forbidden thing, for which I was duly punished."[9]

A TRAGIC FRIENDSHIP

Edgar also excelled in sports, but other boys at his school, now known as Joseph Clarke's Academy, noted that although they respected him for his athletic ability, they were not inclined to become his friends. For his part, Edgar did not seem to reach out for friendships. One classmate, Creed Thomas, recalled later that "It was a noticeable fact that he never asked any of his schoolmates to go home with him after school. Other boys would frequently spend the night or take dinner with each other at their homes, but Poe was seldom known to enter into this social intercourse."[10]

Not only was Edgar an outsider at school, but increasingly he realized that he was not really part of the Allan family. At times, he would take refuge in the homes of his few friends, such as that of Ebenezer Burling. J. H. Whitty notes that "when matters went wrong at Allan's, Edgar hastened to Burling's home, and spent the night there, in opposition to the Allans' wishes."[11]

He also spent time at the home of a classmate, Robert Craig Stanard. Here he developed a youthful crush on a sympathetic adult, Robert's mother, Jane Stith Stanard. To Edgar, the older woman seemed approachable and kind, and he later wrote his famous poem, "To Helen" in her memory.

Stanard was taken from him all too soon, just as his mother had been, by tuberculosis. On April 28, 1824, Jane Stanard died. Her

A Poet in Joseph Clarke's Academy in Richmond, Virginia

Dwight Thomas and David K. Jackson include in The Poe Log *this account of Poe's early interest in poetry and his skills in ancient languages and writing, as recalled later by Edgar's teacher Joseph H. Clarke.*

"Edgar Poe was [several] years in my school. During that time he read Ovid, Caesar, Virgil, Cicero, and Horace in Latin, and Xenophon and Homer in Greek. . . . He had no love for mathematics. . . . While the other boys wrote mere mechanical verses, Poe wrote genuine poetry: the boy was a born poet. As a scholar, he was ambitious to excel, and although not conspicuously studious, he always acquitted himself well in his classes. He was remarkable for self-respect, without haughtiness. In his demeanor toward his playmates, he was strictly just and correct, which made him a general favorite. . . . His natural and predominant passion seemed to me to be an enthusiastic ardor in every-thing he undertook. . . . Even in those early years, Edgar Poe displayed the germs of that wonderfully rich and splendid imagination which has placed him in the front rank of the purely imaginative poets of the world. His school-boy verses were written *con amore* [with love], and not as mere tasks. When he was ten years old, Mr. Allan came to me one day with a manuscript volume of verses, which he said Edgar had written and which the little fellow wanted to have published. He asked my advice upon the subject. I told him that Edgar was of a very excitable temperament, that he possessed a great deal of self-esteem, and that it would be very injurious to the boy to allow him to be flattered and talked about as the author of a printed book at his age. . . . The verses, I remember, consisted chiefly of pieces addressed to the different little girls in Richmond."

memory inspired Edgar, for a while, to make nightly trips to the cemetery to visit her grave. Gradually the pain of losing his friend would fade, but the memory of those trips to visit her grave would stay with him. His poem "Spirits of the Dead," published three years after Stanard died, evokes images of those nighttime visits with the words, "Thy soul shall find itself alone / 'Mid dark thoughts of the gray tomb-stone— / Not one, of all the crowd, to pry / Into thine hour of secrecy."[12]

THE TIES LOOSEN

Meanwhile, Edgar's relationship with his foster father deteriorated, with Allan's attitude changing from standoffishness to annoyance with Edgar's artistic temperament. Allan's declining finances made the situation worse. In 1824, after almost two years without income, Allan sold Ellis his share of the business, and although the Allans continued to live comfortably, Edgar perceived that he would not be in line to inherit what now was a greatly diminished estate. Poe biographer Vincent Buranelli summarizes Edgar's situation with the Allans as living "on the edge of the abyss because they never adopted him."[13]

Also that year, Edgar's older brother Henry, who was working as a sailor on the ship *The Macedonian,* visited Richmond. Upon his return to Baltimore, Henry wrote Edgar a letter, received on October 25, 1824, which Allan saw and responded to almost immediately.

In his letter to Edgar's brother, written on November 1, 1824, Allan revealed the resentment he harbored toward his foster son. In his mind, the blame for the tension between the two lay squarely on fifteen-year-old Edgar's shoulders:

> The boy possesses not a Spark of affection for us, not a particle of gratitude for all my care and kindness towards him. I have given him a much superior Education than ever I received myself. If Rosalie has to relie on any affection from him, God in his mercy preserve her.—I fear his associates have led him to adopt a line of thinking & acting very contrary to what he possessed

when in England. . . . Had I done my duty as faithfully to my God as I have to Edgar, then Death, come when he will, had no terrors for me.[14]

FIRST LOVE

At the same time that tension at home was rising, young Poe was also having to deal with the confusing sensation of being in love, this time with someone his own age. A neighbor of his, Sarah Elmira Royster, had attracted his attention, and soon he was calling on her at home. As was common practice in those days, Edgar would visit with Elmira in her family's formal parlor. There, Elmira would often play the piano for Edgar; sometimes he would draw sketches of her as she played or read aloud the poems he had written for her.

Elmira saw in the young Poe's character a number of contradictions. Years later, in her memoir, she recalled her beau as "beautiful, not very talkative, and sad." Yet, she notes, "Edgar was very generous and warm and zealous, in any cause he was interested in, being enthusiastic and impulsive."[15]

The relationship between Edgar and Elmira was destined to fail, however. Despite the fact that Edgar had grown up in the household of a seemingly prosperous family, Elmira's parents knew of the failure of John Allan's business and held that against Edgar. Moreover, acting was not considered a respectable calling, so the fact that Edgar's parents had been in the theater made him seem to them an unsuitable potential mate for their daughter.

Ignoring her parents' wishes, however, Elmira continued to see Edgar in secret, meeting him often in the garden located between their houses. Within a few months the two were secretly engaged to be married.

FURTHER SCHOOLING

If the future of his relationship with Elmira was cloudy, the future of his relations with John Allan was painfully obvious. In March 1825 William Galt, John Allan's uncle, died and left to Allan a third of his estate, amounting to several hundred thousand dollars. Allan now made it clear that Edgar would not be sharing in the bounty. When his uncle's will became public, Allan immediately spent a good deal of his inheritance on an expensive two-story house in the downtown area of Richmond. For Edgar Allan he bought three pairs of new shoes for $1.50 each. He also paid

Poe, pictured here in a portrait by Samuel Osgood, was described by his first love, Sarah Elmira Royster, as enthusiastic and zealous regarding causes that interested him.

the ten dollars due for his tuition at Joseph Clarke's Academy.

Edgar received one final benefit from Allan's newfound prosperity. Poe had completed his studies under Joseph Clarke and was scholastically prepared to go on to college. The recently established University of Virginia was located in Charlottesville, only a two-hour carriage ride away. Allan gave Edgar $110, and on February 14, 1826, young Poe arrived at the imposing but unfinished campus.

2 Cast upon a Sea of Troubles

John Allan's contribution to Poe's university education proved wholly inadequate. The $110 covered his tuition for only two courses. So Poe chose to enroll in classes in ancient and modern languages and elected not to take mathematics, the course John Allan had specifically told him to take. Even limiting what he spent on tuition, Poe had nearly nothing left to pay for food, room rent, furnishings, clothing, school supplies, and other expenses.

Despite the fact that life at college was a constant struggle just to meet his basic requirements for food and shelter, Poe quickly impressed his two professors with his abilities as a scholar. Poe regularly attended George Long's lectures on Latin authors and distinguished himself by his grasp of the works of Cicero, Virgil, and Horace. George Blaetterman, who taught modern languages, noted equally high achievement on Poe's part, especially in French.

Unable to pay for even his basic needs, much less for minor luxuries and recreation, Poe survived by promising that John Allan would pay for his meals and other day-to-day expenses. Poe, however, had been raised in the lifestyle of the rich youths from old plantation families, and he attempted to win the money he needed to support that lifestyle by playing cards. Unfortunately for him, Poe lost and was soon even deeper in debt. Anticipating the anger he would face from John Allan over incurring these debts, Poe made matters worse by drinking alcohol.

The consequences came quickly. Within a couple of months, by May 1826, Poe's bills had been sent to Allan, who consequently went up to Charlottesville to learn for himself what was going on. What he saw disturbed him. Clearly, the university was still under construction. The library was unfinished, and no books were on its shelves. Worse, the campus was in chaos. Drinking and gambling were common on the part of students; vandalism of university property was obvious; and the student-run government of the university, which was supposed to be keeping order, was largely ineffective.

An Improved Situation

There was little Allan could do about the near anarchy on campus, but he saw to it that Poe's own situation improved somewhat. Allan sent the young man six pairs of socks, a coat, and six yards of cloth for

The Start of Poe's Financial Embarrassment

Jeffrey Meyer in his biography, Edgar Allan Poe: His Life and Legacy, *analyzes Poe's situation in college as one that put Poe at a severe disadvantage in relation to the other students at the University of Virginia.*

"It seems that [John] Allan deliberately sent the seventeen-year-old Poe to the University of Virginia with insufficient funds, knowing full well that this would place him in an impossible situation. It is curious that Allan was willing to provide Poe with an expensive English education when business was bad and he himself had little money, but unwilling to spend less than this amount on Poe's education at Virginia when he possessed a great fortune. Though there were no rational reasons for Allan's behavior, it is possible to speculate on his tortuous motives. He may have resented Poe's assumption that as the son of a wealthy man he would always have plenty of money and wanted to disillusion Poe about this. He may have wished to test Poe's self-sufficiency and see how he would manage on his own (as Allan had to do when he first began to make his way in the world). He may have thought it better for Poe's character to keep him on short funds than spoil him (as he had previously been accused of doing) by undue extravagance. He may have resented (at the same time that he was proud of) Poe's intellectual and artistic ability, and been jealous of his wife's devotion to Poe. He may have unconsciously desired Poe to fail at the university, so that he would not become a professional man—superior to the merchant Allan—but would instead be forced to enter Allan's business and remain under his authority. Finally, he may have wanted to punish Poe for some unspecified offense—quite possibly his criticism of Allan's adultery [generally known in Richmond]. In any case, Allan's attitude toward Poe's higher education clearly reflects a radical change in feeling."

Despite being unable to purchase books and school supplies, Poe quickly impressed his professors at the University of Virginia with his intelligence.

Poe to have made into a suit. Poe thanked Allan in a letter dated May 25, noting that the coat fit perfectly; he also mentioned that he needed some soap and a Latin history book that he had left at home.

In his letter Poe also reported continuing student disturbances, although he was not involved in them. He described injuries of students who had been fighting and noted that the sheriff had been called in to help restore order by conducting an attendance check in the dormitories. In addition, a number of students had been suspended, and one had been expelled.

Over the summer, however, the atmosphere changed for the better. The campus took on a more finished appearance as construction of the library progressed. The faculty took action to strengthen the academic standards by announcing that general examinations would be administered in December. These exams would include first-year and second-year students alike, which meant that every student would have to start taking coursework more seriously. In his letter of September 21, 1826, Poe expressed concern over the faculty's decision, although he noted he was making the best of his circumstances by studying harder:

> Tho' it will hardly be fair to examine those who have only been here one session, with those who have been here two—and some of whom have come from other colleges—still I suppose I shall have to stand my examination with the rest—
>
> I have been studying a great deal in order to be prepared, and dare say I shall come off as well as the rest of them, that

is—if I don't get frightened—Perhaps you will have some business up here about that time, and then you can judge for yourself—[16]

Poe's biographer William Bittner notes that the young man's hard work paid off: "He read a volume of Voltaire and an anthology and drill book on French, [and when the examination] results were announced, Poe stood in the second rank in Latin . . . and in the first in French."[17]

BACK IN THE ALLAN HOME

After the announcement of the results of the examinations, Allan went up again to the university, this time to fetch Poe home for the end of the term and the December holidays. Presented with debts that amounted to nearly twenty-five hundred dollars, Allan "paid every debt that he thought ought to be paid,"[18] and then put Poe to work to help repay the money he had spent. Poe was assigned to help out with the bookkeeping and correspondence still to be done in the settlement of the Ellis and Allan tobacco trading business.

Poe's employment as a bookkeeper did nothing to improve his relationship with his foster father. Allan's self-righteous attitude ran up against Poe's own adolescent rebelliousness and his lack of interest in the failed business. Allan intensified his efforts to discipline Poe, who, in return, chafed under restraints that seemed to him either retaliatory or arbitrary.

Adding to Poe's unhappiness was the end of his relationship with Elmira Royster. In the months Poe had been away at the

The Mongol conqueror known as Tamerlane was the subject of Poe's poem "Tamerlane."

appointing to Allan was the realization that young Poe had no interest in earning a living in business but wanted to pursue a literary career. When he was not working at his bookkeeping, Poe was polishing a narrative poem he had been writing. "Tamerlane" was loosely based on the story of the Mongol conqueror known as Tamerlane, who in 1402 defeated the Turks in the Battle of Angora. In Poe's version of the story, Tamerlane is on his deathbed and speaks of his remorse for having allowed ambition to separate him from his childhood sweetheart.

But the real breaking point in Poe's relationship with John Allan came on the day when Frances Allan finally discovered what her neighbors had known for some time: that her husband had been unfaithful and that Edwin Collier was Allan's illegitimate son. In the ensuing confrontation over Allan's infidelity, Poe sided with his foster mother; as a result, Allan's anger fell on Poe. He charged the youth with idleness, told him he would grant no more money for a university education, and ordered him to leave the house. Poe complied with Allan's order, and the next day sent him a letter in which he took responsibility for the breakup and declared that his departure was permanent.

> Sir,
>
> After my treatment on yesterday and what passed between us this morning, I can hardly think you will be surprised at the contents of this letter. My determination is at length taken—to leave your house and endeavor to find some place in this wide world, where I will be treated—not as *you* have treated me—

university, Elmira had become engaged to another suitor, Alexander Shelton. Many years later Elmira revealed in her memoir that her father had played a part in driving a wedge between herself and Poe: "[D]uring the time [Edgar] was at the University he wrote to me frequently, but my father intercepted the letters because we were too young—for no other reason. . . . I was about 15 or 16 when he first addressed me and I engaged myself to him, and I was not aware that he wrote to me until I was married to Mr. Shelton when I was 17."[19]

FINAL SEPARATION

Over the next three months, tensions at the Allan home continued to mount. Most dis-

A University Without Discipline

When Poe attended college, the librarian at the University of Virginia was William Wertenbaker. Wertenbaker recounted to Poe's biographer John H. Ingram some of the difficulties caused by a lack of discipline at the university, where founder Thomas Jefferson had decreed that everything was supposed to be run by the students. His account is included in Edgar Allan Poe: His Life, Letters and Opinions.

"The session of 1825 was commenced without any discipline at all, and without an effort on the part of the Faculty to enforce obedience to the laws. They were expecting and waiting for the students to inaugurate Mr. Jefferson's system of self-government, but this they resolutely refused to do. Neither the entreaties of Mr. Jefferson, nor the persuasion of the professors, could induce a single student to accept the office of Censor. The plan was that a Board of Censors, consisting of six of the most discreet students, should inquire into the facts in all cases of minor offenses, and name the punishment which they thought proportioned to the offense.

In this state of affairs, and for several months, insubordination, lawlessness, and riot ruled the institution, and became so intolerable to the professors that they suspended operations, and tendered their resignations to the Board of Visitors. The Board met immediately; abandoned the plan of self-government; enacted new laws; ordered a course of rigid discipline to be pursued, and invested the Faculty with full authority to rule and govern the institution.

In exercising the power now granted them, the Faculty (as in the circumstances it was quite natural for them to do) perhaps erred in going to the opposite extreme of punishing offenders with too great severity."

Thomas Jefferson intended for students of the University of Virginia to govern themselves, but the plan was eventually abandoned.

This is not a hurried determination, but one on which I have long considered— and having so considered my resolution is unalterable—You may perhaps think that I have flown off in a passion, & that I am already wishing to return; But not so—I will give you the reasons which have actuated me, and then judge [for yourself]—.[20]

Poe also noted what he saw as a great injustice; that Allan wanted him to succeed but then denied him the very means to attain his goals by withholding money to pay his tuition:

Since I have been able to think on any subject, my thoughts have aspired, and they have been taught by *you* to aspire, to eminence in public life—and this cannot be attained without a good Education, such a one I cannot obtain at a Primary school—A collegiate Education therefore was what I most ardently desired, and I had been led to expect that it would at some future time be granted—but in a moment of caprice—you have blasted my hope because forsooth I disagreed with you in an opinion, which opinion I was forced to express—Again, I have heard you say (when you little thought I was listening and therefore must have said it in earnest) that you had no affection for me.[21]

Poe expressed a final grievance against Allan. Allan had apparently put Poe in a position of having to take orders from one or more of the household slaves. For a young white man in 1820s' Virginia, that was a particular affront, as Poe noted: "You suffer me to be subjected to the whims & caprice, not only of your white family, but the complete authority of the blacks— these grievances I could not submit to; and I am gone."[22] Poe also asked for his trunk and a small amount of money to be sent to him at a local hotel where he was staying.

Allan did not respond to this letter nor to one Poe sent the next day saying that he was hungry. However, one of the servants brought him a bundle of his clothing, and, by the end of a week, someone—perhaps Frances Allan—sent him enough money to buy a passage on a boat headed for Boston.

A BOSTONIAN

Alone in Boston, and continuing to write poetry, Poe experienced the misery of homelessness, hunger, and unrewarded labor at dead-end jobs. He first used his experience in Allan's office to find a job as a clerk in a wholesale house. Here he was cheated out of his wages, and as a result he soon was thrown out of his room for not paying his rent.

For nearly two months, Poe tried to earn money by writing. Although he failed to land any full-time jobs, he did manage to convince Calvin F. S. Thomas of Boston to print fifty copies of his forty-page volume titled *Tamerlane and Other Poems*, listing its author only as "a Bostonian."

Desperate for money, he told one friend of his that his last resort was to join the army, and on May 26, 1827, he used the pseudonym Edgar A. Perry to enlist. In the register of enlistments Poe described himself as having grey eyes, brown hair, fair complexion, and a height of five feet and

AN EXCELLENT STUDENT AND AGREEABLE HOST

James A. Harrison in his seventeen-volume The Complete Works of Edgar Allan Poe, *includes this recollection of Poe written in 1869 by the University of Virginia librarian, William Wertenbaker.*

"Mr. Poe was a student during the second session, which commenced February 1st, and terminated December 15th, 1826. He signed the matriculation book on the 14th of February, and remained in good standing until the session closed. He was born on the 19th day of January, 1809, being a little over seventeen when he matriculated. He entered the school of Ancient and Modern Languages, attending the lectures on Latin, Greek, French, Spanish, and Italian.

I was a member of the last three classes, and can testify that he was tolerably regular in his attendance and a successful student, having obtained distinction at the final examination in Latin and French, and this was at the time the highest honour a student could obtain. . . .

On one occasion Professor Blaettermann requested his Italian class to render into English verse a portion of the lesson in [the Italian Renaissance poet] Tasso, which he had assigned them for the next lecture. He did not require this of them as a regular class exercise, but recommended it as one from which he thought the students would derive benefit. At the next lecture on Italian the Professor stated from his chair that Mr. Poe was the only member of the class who had responded to his suggestion, and paid a very high compliment to his performance.

As Librarian I had frequent official intercourse with Mr. Poe, but it was at or near the close of the session before I met him in the social circle. After spending an evening together at a private house, he invited me in on our return to his room. It was a cold night in December, and his fire having gone pretty nearly out, by the aid of some tallow candles, and the fragments of a small table which he broke up for the purpose, he soon rekindled it, and by its comfortable blaze I spent a very pleasant hour with him. On this occasion he spoke with regret of the large amount of money he had wasted and of the debts he had contracted during the session."

eight inches. He was committed to five years of service as part of Battery H of the First Artillery in Fort Independence, located in Boston Harbor.

To the Allan family, Poe seemed to have disappeared completely. In a brief speculation as to what could have happened to him, John Allan wrote to his sister, "I'm thinking Edgar has gone to Sea to seek his own fortunes."[23]

Tamerlane and Other Poems came out that summer. Poe had the pleasure of reading a notice of its publication in the *United States Review,* a literary magazine published in Boston. However, only a few copies sold.

ARMY LIFE

Poe's first summer in the army was spent routinely, mostly at standing guard duty. At the end of October he was reassigned to Fort Moultrie, on Sullivan's Island off the coast of Charleston, South Carolina, where he remained on duty for a year.

Before long, Poe found himself freed of guard duty, and by December 1828, it appeared that Poe was making a success of himself as a clerk in the army, using the skills he had learned in the Allan business. Biographer Hervey Allen notes: "Poe's duties evidently brought him into close con-

When Poe enlisted in the army under the name of Edgar A. Perry, he was first assigned to Fort Independence in Boston Harbor.

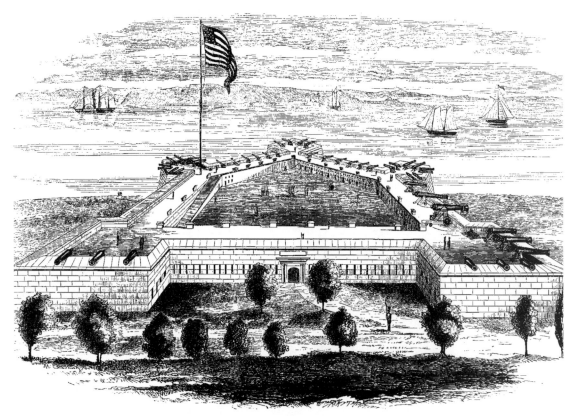

When Poe was transferred in the late 1820s to Fort Monroe, Virginia—shown here as it appeared in 1862— he realized he had to reveal his true identity.

tact with his officers. He was steady, sober, and intelligent; and promotion ensued. We soon find him listed as an 'artifacer' [a type of clerk], the first step out of the ranks."[24]

Life as an army recruit, however, did not suit Poe, despite having free time to write poetry, read, or take walks along the beaches. Feeling that he was wasting his life on routine, boring duties, he expressed his frustrations to his superior officer, Lieutenant J. Howard, who encouraged Poe to seek officers' training.

Making the transition to officers' training involved some complications, however. For one thing, Poe's true identity had come to light when he was recognized by an acquaintance from his university days. Moreover, he was slated to be transferred to Fort Monroe, located just outside of Richmond, where it was almost certain that others would recognize him as well. Poe therefore decided to reveal to his commanding officer his identity and the facts of his separation from John Allan.

With the resumption of his own name, Poe began hearing news that neither of the Allans was in good health. Poe's commanding officer had already told him that he should seek reconciliation with John Allan. So, on December 1, 1828, Poe wrote to Allan explaining that he needed his foster father's permission to cut his enlistment short and move into officers' training:

> I have been in the American army as long as suits my ends or my inclination, and it is now time that I should leave it—To this effect I made known my circumstances to Lieut. Howard who promised me my discharge solely upon a re-conciliation with yourself—In vain I told him that your wishes for me (as your letters assured me) were, and had always been those of a father & that you were ready to forgive even the worst offences—He insisted upon my writing you & that if a re-conciliation could be effected he would grant me my wish— This was advised in the goodness of his heart & with a view of serving me in a double sense—He has always been kind to me, and, in my respect, reminds me forcibly of yourself. . . .
>
> You need not fear for my future prosperity—I am altered from what you knew me, & am no longer a boy tossing about on the world without aim or consistency—I feel that within me which will make me fulfill your highest wishes & only beg you to suspend your judgement until you hear *of* me again. . . .
>
> Write me once more if you do really forgive me [and] let me know how my Ma preserves her health. . . . I hope she will not let my wayward disposition wear away the love she used to have for me.[25]

John Allan did not reply to this letter nor to two others Poe wrote. By the end of February 1829, Poe had been at Fort Monroe for nearly two months and had been promoted to the rank of sergeant major. Still John Allan remained silent.

Clearly, John Allan had decided that there should be no reconciliation. Poe's biographer Hervey Allen notes that John Allan had gone so far as to keep Poe away even against his dying wife's wishes:

> Strange as it may seem, John Allan remained firm until the very last. He finally sent for his foster-son, then only a few miles away from Richmond, but it was too late. Mrs. Allan died before Poe arrived home, and despite her dying request not to be buried until her foster-son returned, her husband proceeded with the funeral. When Poe arrived at the house a few hours later, all that he loved most was in the ground. His agony at the grave is said to have been extreme.[26]

THE STRUGGLE TO ENTER WEST POINT

Following Frances Allan's funeral, and despite Allan's coolness, a reconciliation of sorts took place. Allan helped Poe to pay another recruit to complete the remaining three years of his enlistment—a common practice at the time. Having declared he wanted to be an officer and been freed of his obligations as a recruit, Poe returned to Richmond and set about obtaining an appointment to the U.S. Military Academy at West Point.

Admission to West Point required passing examinations and obtaining an appointment from the War Department. Before a month had gone by, Poe realized he had too many distractions in Richmond to allow him to study for the examinations. Thinking also that he could perhaps speed up the appointment by being closer to Washington, D.C., Poe moved to Baltimore, which was near Washington and home to a number of his relatives.

On his first opportunity, he visited the nearby city of Washington. There he found that his grandfather's service to the Revolutionary army was still remembered and that these memories translated into at least a little recognition for Poe. On May 20, 1829, he wrote to Allan from Baltimore that he had called on U.S. Attorney General William Wirt, who "treated me with great politeness and invited me to call & see him frequently while I stay in Baltimore—I have called upon him several times [and] have been introduced to many gentlemen of high standing in the city, who were formerly acquainted with my grandfather."[27]

While he was living in Baltimore, Poe called upon Attorney General William Wirt (pictured) who treated him politely and invited him to visit often.

LITERARY AMBITIONS

As it happened, Wirt also had a reputation as a biographer. Taking advantage of his new friend's literary experience, Poe asked Wirt to look over his newest composition, another narrative poem entitled "Al Aaraaf." Wirt was kind enough to read the manuscript and to write Poe an encouraging letter, which Poe forwarded to Isaac Lea of the publishing house Lea and Carey, along with the poem and a revision of the volume he had published anonymously in Boston two years earlier.

"Al Aaraaf" is set on the suddenly appearing star observed by the astronomer Tycho Brahe in 1572. In this celestial setting are some sixteenth-century personages who, Poe said, "would not be pleased with an immortality even of bliss"[28] and who are enjoying a fleeting happiness in this bright but temporary star world.

In addition to approaching Lea and Carey, Poe wrote to Allan, asking him for one hundred dollars so he could print his poem privately. Not surprisingly, Allan declined to send the money and advised that Poe concentrate on getting into West Point.

Despite the positive comments of William Wirt, Lea and Carey refused to publish Poe's manuscript. Undeterred, he went on to submit it to the publisher Hatch and Dunning of Baltimore. This time the manuscript was accepted, and Poe signed his name to it. *Al Aaraaf, Tamerlane and Minor Poems,* a small hardbound book numbering seventy-one pages, came out in an edition of 250 copies.

Reviewers took note of this 1829 volume. One well-known critic, John Jill Hewitt, was unimpressed, but an anonymous reviewer in *American Ladies' Magazine and Literary Gazette,* while mentioning Poe's youth, lack of judgment, and experience, also favorably compared Poe to a famous Romantic poet, saying that parts of the book "remind us of no less a poet than [Percy Bysshe] Shelley." And the influential reviewer John Neal in Portland, Maine, predicted that the young author "will be *foremost* in the rank of *real* poets."[29]

THE POE RELATIONS

While Poe worked on his poetry and awaited his appointment to West Point, he became further acquainted with his relatives in Baltimore. Not all his kinsmen were pleased to see him. One cousin, Neilson Poe, was convinced that Edgar, by antagonizing Allan, had lost out on a fortune. After he read the reviewer John Neal's assessment, however, Neilson softened somewhat and even commented that Edgar would bring fame to the family.

Among the Poes living in Baltimore was his youngest aunt, Maria Poe Clemm, who was boarding several other members of the Poe family in her home: Edgar's own older brother Henry Poe, his grandmother Elizabeth Cairnes Poe, Maria's son Henry Clemm, and her daughter, nine-year-old Virginia Maria Clemm.

The entire household lived in poverty. Although Maria Poe Clemm brought in a little money as a schoolteacher and later as a seamstress, the household relied for sustenance on the annual $240 government pension that Elizabeth Cairnes Poe received as the widow of a Revolutionary War veteran. In spite of the scarcity of

Cadets marching at the U.S. Military Academy at West Point, circa 1820. Once enrolled in 1830, Poe quickly determined that West Point was not for him.

money, Clemm paid her nephew from time to time for tutoring the child Virginia.

THE REALITY OF WEST POINT

For fourteen months Poe waited for his appointment to the U.S. Military Academy. John Allan provided support by sending four much-needed blankets and small sums of money to Baltimore. Upon Poe's acceptance to West Point at the end of May 1830, Allan gave him another fifty dollars. Poe then moved to West Point in the latter part of June.

By June 28, 1830, he had passed the qualifying examinations and had settled into his academic studies and the rigid routine of duties as a West Point cadet. Predictably, Poe did well in the midterm examinations, ranking seventeenth in mathematics and third in French in a class of 91 cadets.

But as much as Poe enjoyed his studies at West Point, he was noted by fellow cadet Alan B. Magruder and others as not being suited for officers' training. Magruder noted that Poe's "wayward and capricious temper made him at times utterly oblivious or indifferent to the ordinary routine of roll-calls, drills, and guard duties."[30] But he was popular with the other cadets, who enjoyed Poe's humor, for he had a biting wit, which he used in private, mocking the officers who ran West Point.

Just as army life had, life at West Point soon soured for Poe. He found that his studies left him much less time for writing than he had had as an army recruit. Poe's dissatisfaction was so obvious that Colonel Sylvanus Thayer, the academy's superintendent, counseled him to leave West Point.

Again, there was a problem. A release from his duties would be granted only with John Allan's blessing. Once more, Poe wrote for Allan's permission to leave his military post. As before, Allan did not respond.

This time, Poe decided to seek a court-martial, and thus dismissal, by neglecting his regular duties. The formal accusations were quickly brought against him, and at the end of January he pleaded guilty to absenting himself from all parades, roll calls, classes, and church attendance beginning January 8. Poe's dismissal from West Point was approved by John Henry Eaton, U.S. secretary of war, and he was released on February 18, 1831.

Poe left West Point the next day with few clothes and no cloak and only twenty-four cents in his pocket. He arrived in New York with a bad cold, and once again he appealed to John Allan for help, writing,

> I have no money—no friends—I have written to my brother—but he cannot help me—I shall never rise from my bed—besides a most violent cold on my lungs, my *ear* discharges blood and matter continually and my headache is distracting—I hardly know what I am writing—I will write no more—Please send me a little money—quickly—and forget what I said about you.[31]

MORE INTIMATIONS OF SUCCESS

Poe heard nothing from John Allan, but fortunately his symptoms eased, and he was soon well enough to go about trying to find a publisher for the latest revision of his collection of poems. When he found a publisher, Poe sent word to Colonel Thayer at West Point that his book would be dedicated to the cadets and that copies could be reserved by individuals for $1.25. Several officers and 131 cadets contributed by payroll deduction the amount he asked, and this volume, signed and entitled simply *Poems*, came off the press in April 1831. The academy treasurer Thomas J. Leslie issued to him his payment of $170.

Poe's West Point readers were disappointed, however, for no humorous characterizations of academy officers were in the book. Although the West Point cadets felt let down, the reviewers were encouraging. With its much improved version of "Tamerlane," *Poems* was favorably received by James Watson Webb of the *Morning Courier and New York Enquirer*. In addition, the *New York Mirror* quoted the poems "The Doomed City" and "Fairy Land" in the May 7 edition.

TROUBLES MULTIPLY

Poe also looked for work in New York, but he was unsuccessful. With no money and no place else to go, he moved back to Baltimore to stay with his aunt, Maria Clemm.

A Cry of Distress

Poe was not above begging for money, even from those he had come to despise. This letter from Poe to John Allan, dated December 15, 1831, exhibits how Poe was willing to swallow his pride when asking for help. It is printed in The Letters of Edgar Allan Poe, *edited by John Ward Ostrom.*

"Dear Pa,

I am sure you could not refuse to assist me if you were well aware of the distress I am in. How often have you relieved the distresses of a perfect stranger in circumstances less urgent than mine, and yet when I beg and intreat you in the name of God to send me succour you will still refuse to aid me. I know that I have offended you past all forgiveness, and I know that I have no longer any hopes of being again received into your favour, but, for the sake of Christ, do not let me perish for a sum of money which you would never miss, and which would relieve me from the greatest earthly misery. . . . Oh! if you knew at this moment how wretched I am you would never forgive yourself for having refused me. You are enjoying yourself in all the blessings that wealth & happiness can bestow, and I am suffering every extremity of want and misery without even a chance of escape, or a friend to whom I can look up to for assistance.

Think for one moment, and if your nature and former heart are not altogether changed you will not longer refuse me assistance if not for my sake for the sake of humanity.

I know that you have never turned a beggar from your door, and I apply to you in that light, I *beg* you for a little aid, and for the sake of all that was formerly dear to you I trust that you will relieve me.

If you wish me to humble myself before you I am humble—Sickness and misfortune have left me not a shadow of pride. I own that I am miserable and unworthy of your notice, but do not leave me to perish without leaving me still one resource. I feel at the very bottom of my heart that if you were in my situation and you in mine, how differently I would act.

Yours affect[ionately]
E A P."

There he found that his brother was very ill with tuberculosis.

Henry died on August 1 and was buried on August 3, 1831. Treating Henry Poe's illness and paying for his funeral left the family destitute, forcing Edgar once more to beg Allan on November 18, 1831, for money—this time eighty dollars to cover "a debt which I never expected to have to pay, and which was incurred as much on Henry's account as my own."[32] Allan did not reply to this nor to two other letters of distress dated December 15 and December 29, 1831.

Yet Poe was looking with renewed hope toward the new year. After months of working in obscurity, he believed that he had found a way not only to make his writing pay but to get it into the hands of the reading public.

Chapter

3 Richmond Journalist and Family Man

Poe was experimenting with a genre and outlet that were new to him. After years of writing poetry, he had decided to try writing fiction for magazines. A weekly paper in Philadelphia, the *Saturday Courier,* was sponsoring a short-story contest, and the first prize was to be one hundred dollars.

Poe submitted five tales to the contest: "Metzengerstein," "Duke de L'Omelette," "A Tale of Jerusalem," "A Decided Loss," and "The Bargain Lost." Poe considered these stories to be part of a series he called *Tales of the Folio Club.* The tales satirized the work of the Delphian Club, whose members were prominent in Baltimore's literary community. Poe was poking fun not just at the authors who met monthly to read and critique each others' stories, but also at literary critics in the club.

None of the stories won the prize, but all were published by the *Saturday Courier.* In addition, "The Duke de L'Omelette" appeared in two other magazines. Poe was gratified that his work was being read, and he made the rounds of his Baltimore relatives to bask in the limelight of modest fame. However, Poe received no money, since, according to the rules of the contest, all five stories had become the property of the *Saturday Courier.*

ANOTHER CONTEST

Throughout 1832, Poe worked on additional Folio Club satires, still hoping that his efforts would pay off in the form of money for him. In the early part of 1833, Lambert A. Wilmer, who had been a friend of Poe's brother and who was editor of the Baltimore *Saturday Visitor,* took notice of his writing. Wilmer accepted several of Poe's poems in the spring of 1833. Then, in June 1833, Wilmer announced a *Saturday Visitor* contest similar to the one the *Saturday Courier* had run in Philadelphia. This time, Poe won the first prize of fifty dollars, with another tale from the Folio Club series, "MS. Found in a Bottle." His poem "The Coliseum" won second place in the poetry contest, although no prize money was involved.

The judges of the contest, John Latrobe and John Pendleton Kennedy, were both well connected among publishers, so Poe immediately sought their help in getting the entire series of Folio Club tales published. Latrobe, in particular, was impressed by Poe. To him, the young author seemed a man of education and poise:

His figure was remarkably good, and he carried himself erect and well, as one who had been trained to it. He

Even as a struggling journalist, Poe presented himself well, appearing confident and poised.

Both Latrobe and Kennedy took an interest in Poe and convinced Wilmer to announce that *Tales of the Folio Club* would be published on subscription; that is, a copy of the book would be sent to each individual reader who agreed to pay for it. Poe turned down the offer, however, and instead asked Kennedy to take the manuscript to Lea and Carey in Philadelphia. That initiative was a failure. Recalling, perhaps, the poor reception Poe's poems had received with the reading public, Lea and Carey declined to publish the collection, and for two months they did not even acknowledge receiving the manuscript.

LAST VISIT TO JOHN ALLAN

Poe was trying to establish himself, but even as he showed signs of achieving modest success in his chosen career, he continued to pursue a relationship with John Allan. During the winter, upon learning that Allan was incapacitated with a form of heart disease known at the time as dropsy, Poe made the trip from Baltimore to Richmond in one last attempt to be reconciled with his foster father. On February 14, 1834, he went to the house and rang the bell. Allan's second wife, Louisa Patterson Allan, answered the door. Thomas H. Ellis, the son of Allan's former business partner, later recalled what happened:

> a man of remarkable appearance . . . asked [her] if he could see Mr. Allan. She replied that Mr. Allan's condition was such that his physicians had pro-

was dressed in black, and his frockcoat was buttoned at the throat, where it met the black stock, then almost universally worn. Not a particle of white was visible. Coat, hat, boots and gloves had very evidently seen their best days, but so far as mending and brushing go, everything had been done apparently, to make them presentable. On most men his clothes would have looked shabby and seedy, but there was something about this man that prevented one from criticizing his garments.[33]

hibited any person from seeing him except his nurses. The man was Edgar A. Poe, who was, of course, perfectly familiar with the house. Thrusting her aside & without noticing her reply, he passed rapidly upstairs to Mr. Allan's chamber, followed by Mrs. Allan. As soon as he entered the chamber, Mr. Allan raised his cane, & threatened to strike him if he came within reach, ordered him out; upon which Poe withdrew, & that was the last time they ever met.[34]

John Allan died just a few weeks later, on March 27, 1834. Edgar Allan Poe was not even mentioned in Allan's will.

NEW CONTACT IN RICHMOND

With Allan's death, Poe had to accept the fact that he was on his own financially. That fall, at Kennedy's recommendation, he started sending his works to a new magazine getting under way in his hometown of Richmond, Virginia. This was the *Southern Literary Messenger*, owned by Thomas H. White. Over the next few months, White published several of Poe's submissions, including a horror story titled "Berenice," a poem, "To Mary," and a couple of literary reviews.

Poe took a personal interest in the new literary journal, and in long letters to White suggested how the fledgling paper

---

TALES OF THE FOLIO CLUB

As a freelance writer, Poe was forced to market his own stories to the publishers. In this letter to the editors of the New England Magazine, *printed in* The Letters of Edgar Allan Poe, *edited by John Ward Ostrom, he submits his tale "Epimanes," along with a synopsis of his series,* Tales of the Folio Club.

"I send you an original tale in hope of your accepting it for the *New England Magazine*. It is one of a number of similar pieces which I have contemplated publishing under the title of 'Eleven Tales of the Arabesque.' They are supposed to be read at table by the eleven members of a literary club, and are followed by the remarks of the company upon each. These remarks are intended as a burlesque upon criticism. In the whole, originality more than any thing else has been attempted. I have said this much with a view of offering you the entire Manuscript. If you like the specimen which I have sent I will forward the rest at your suggestion—but if you decide upon publishing all the tales, it would not be proper to print the one I now send until it can be printed in its place with the others. It is however optional with you whether to accept them at all, or publish 'Epimanes' and reject the rest—if indeed you do not reject them altogether."

might be publicized. As a result, Poe earned a little money by writing advertisements on behalf of the *Messenger* for several other magazines.

Poe's opportunity to advance his career further presented itself the next spring. When the editor of the *Messenger* resigned, White offered to let Poe try out for the job. Poe quickly accepted. In a letter written June 22, 1835, Poe let White know that "nothing would give me greater pleasure" than coming to Richmond, "for at present a very small portion of my time is employed."[35] No sooner was Poe at work at the *Messenger* than the magazine began to carry his stories as well as his reviews of a wide variety of books.

WORKING ON THE *SOUTHERN LITERARY MESSENGER*

From the time of Poe's arrival in Richmond, White gave him a great deal of writing responsibility. Because it was a literary magazine, the *Messenger*'s space was mostly devoted to reviews of new books submitted by publishers, who hoped that

---

SUCCESS ON THE *SOUTHERN LITERARY MESSENGER*

A month before Poe left the Southern Literary Messenger, *its owner, Thomas H. White, was having trouble with his editor. Judge Beverly Tucker, who had offered his assistance to the paper before Poe came, received evidence of White's impatience in this letter, which is quoted in* The Poe Log, *edited by Dwight Thomas and David K. Jackson.*

"Highly as I really think of Mr. Poe's talents, I shall be forced to give him notice, in a week or so at farthest, that I can no longer recognize him as editor of my *Messenger*. Three months ago I felt it my duty to give him a similar notice,—and was afterwards overpersuaded to restore him to his situation on certain conditions—which conditions he has again forfeited. Added to all this, I am cramped by him in the exercise of my own judgment, as to what articles I shall or shall not admit into my work. It is true that I neither have his sagacity, nor his learning—but I do believe I know a handspike from a saw. . . . I mean to dispense with Mr. Poe as my editor . . . if he chooses to write as a contributor, I will pay him well."

Just over a month later, in another letter to Tucker, White expressed even greater exasperation:

"Poe pesters me no little. . . . He is continually after me for money. I am as sick of his writings, as I am of him,—and am rather more than half inclined to send him up another dozen dollars in the morning, and along with it all his unpublished manuscripts."

Poe's return to Richmond, Virginia (pictured), for a trial run as editor of the Southern Literary Messenger *not only reintroduced him to Richmond society but also to the use of alcohol.*

favorable assessments would help sales of new titles. Poe threw himself into this labor with vigor.

Besides finding satisfaction in analyzing the authors' strengths and weaknesses, Poe took pleasure in the power he now wielded. Biographer William Bittner notes:

> It was a tremendous satisfaction, after eight years of struggle, finally to be a professional literary man. The editorial offices that he had addressed, sometimes timidly, sometimes exuberantly, faded in importance at the thought of his own editorial desk. Here the manuscripts of hopeful authors would come, and the books for review. Even though he was on the other side of the fence now, he remembered the suspense of waiting for an answer. . . .

It was a social triumph, too, to be back in Richmond. There were many old friends to see, and Southern hospitality flowed freely for the "wastrel" who had surprised his friends as well as his foes by breaking into prominence in the world of letters.[36]

Although White was taking him only on trial, Poe felt himself to be the magazine's official editor. Not only had he published several pieces of his own in the *Messenger,* but he had received favorable notices in other magazines for some of those works.

Unfortunately, the problem Poe had suffered from during his university days dogged him once again as he enjoyed socializing with other members of Richmond society. He had no tolerance for alcohol, so a single glass of wine would make him drunk. On miserable mornings after taking a drink, he would try to deal with hangovers by taking still more alcohol. It was only a few weeks before White, who disapproved of all drinking, withdrew his offer of the editorship. Once again, Poe was jobless and forced to move on.

First Job as Editor

Returning to Baltimore, Poe found his aunt and cousin Virginia in financial straits. His grandmother, Elizabeth Cairnes Poe, had died recently and with her death the government pension upon which the Clemms had depended came to an end. Needing money, Poe wrote to White to ask for his job back, promising that he would not drink.

White offered hope of reinstatement but made it clear that he would not tolerate any use of alcohol. "You have fine talents, Edgar," wrote White, "and you ought to have them respected as well as yourself. Learn to respect yourself, and you will very soon find that you are respected. Separate yourself from the bottle, and bottle-companions, for ever!"[37]

Meanwhile White had published a number of Poe's works that he had on hand. The September issue of his paper contained Poe's tales "Loss of Breath" and "King Pest the First," the poems "Lines Written in an Album" and "Shadow," in addition to a number of his critical notices and reviews. These works attracted the attention of others in the local literary community. A columnist for the *Richmond Compiler* wrote: "For God's sake, value [Poe] according to his merits, which are exceeding great. I say

this with deliberation, for I have been months in coming to the conclusion that he is the first genius, in his line, in Virginia."[38]

White now officially made Poe his editor, offering him five hundred dollars a year to oversee the sixty-four-page monthly magazine. On October 3, 1835, Poe moved back to Richmond, bringing with him Maria Clemm and Virginia, who was now thirteen years of age. The family moved into a boardinghouse in Richmond, and Poe began a period of sobriety and immense literary output that lasted for several months.

Prolific Writer

The *Messenger* immediately became a major outlet for Poe's work. The December issue contained his story "MS. Found in a Bottle," along with twenty-one brief literary critiques. By February he had published eleven more of his stories. Dozens more of his caustic, interesting, and carefully worded literary reviews appeared as well. The result, Poe biographer William Bittner says, was that "the world began to notice the magazine. . . . Circulation began to go up, and White . . . gave him a raise of two dollars a week."[39]

Married to Virginia

By the spring of 1836, Poe seemed to have established himself in Richmond. Now he began to look into other aspects of his life. In particular, he began to take a romantic interest in his cousin, Virginia Clemm. Virginia, at age fourteen, was not mature in either looks or mannerisms, but she was a beautiful girl with large, liquid brown eyes and dark hair set off by her pale complexion.

The relationship between Poe and Virginia developed quickly. On May 16, 1836, Maria Clemm went with Poe to the courthouse and lied about Virginia's age to the magistrate so that the couple could be married. After a modest wedding luncheon at the boardinghouse and an overnight honeymoon, Edgar Allan Poe and his young wife became part of Richmond society.

Although Poe had been supporting Clemm and Virginia before the marriage,

Virginia Clemm was fourteen years old when she married Edgar Allan Poe in 1836.

their needs now came to the attention of White. As a way of helping his new editor, White offered to buy a house that Clemm could use to take in boarders. White himself would be the first of these.

With high hopes for the future of his family, Poe bought furniture on a two hundred-dollar-loan. But the investment turned out to be a poor one. Poe had found no time to look at the house before the purchase was completed, and now he found the dining room was too small to accommodate even one boarder besides White. With only one boarder, the income was inadequate to make payments on the loan.

TENSION BUILDS

In addition to his daily duties, Poe continued to expand his literary horizons. Still hopeful about prospects of getting *Tales of the Folio Club* published, Poe approached Harper and Brothers in New York. Although they declined to publish the collection, they did offer encouragement by suggesting that he write a novel. Following up on this idea, he began work on a book he titled *The Narrative of Arthur Gordon Pym*, the horrific story of a sailor's bad luck on a fictional voyage into the uncharted South Seas.

Pym was an expression of Poe's fascination with seafaring lore and disasters as well as a vehicle for his satiric wit. The story of an expedition to Antarctica, supposedly told by Pym before he died, is a strange mix of realism and spoof designed to evoke fear and wonder. But although humor is an element of this work, scholar Paul Lewis notes that humor fails to tri-

umph over fear: repeatedly, in the course of "[Pym's] quest for knowledge, creatures, people, and things that had seemed familiar or amusing change or reveal themselves to be savage, monstrous, and dangerous."[40]

Despite the professional success Poe was enjoying, there were signs of trouble. White, concerned about the caustic tone of many of Poe's reviews, began to attempt more direct control over Poe's work, and the resulting tension began to wear on both men. Money also became an issue. Bittner writes that "both White and Poe were dissatisfied and cagey with each other, and neither forgot that Edgar's salary was due to go up five dollars a week in November."[41] White began to complain that nobody in Richmond had any money and that the printers were on strike. For his part, Poe began to think that White was planning to replace him as editor.

HIGH HOPES FOR NEW YORK CITY

Whether or not White was actually planning to sack his editor, Poe never gave him the chance. With confidence and ambition fed by the wide recognition his name was now getting, Poe resigned from the *Messenger* at the beginning of 1837. He left for the January and February issues his first two installments of *Pym* and moved north once again.

By February 28, 1837, Poe and his family were in New York City with high expectations of professional success. Thanks

In 1837 Poe felt fame was within reach when he was invited to give a toast at a Booksellers Dinner attended by many in the New York literary community, including short-story writer Washington Irving (pictured here).

to his *Messenger* reviews, Poe was already well known to many members of the New York literary community, and he was sure that meeting these individuals would advance his career. Being invited to give a toast at the annual Booksellers Dinner, which many of these same people attended, heightened his hopes for success. Sharing the table with such highly regarded men of letters as the poet William Cullen Bryant and the short-story writer Washington Irving, in Poe's mind at least, seemed to put fame within reach.

MAKING IT IN A NEW PLACE

Still, the promise of fame did not put money in Poe's pocket. Since her nephew lacked a job, Maria Clemm tried to bring in some cash to pay for their necessities. For the eight months the Poes lived in New York during 1837, Clemm managed the boardinghouse they occupied. One of the other boarders, William Gowans, an influential bookseller, became their appreciative friend. Gowans acquainted the family with the neighborhood and introduced Poe to the book lovers he knew.

Meanwhile, Poe kept at his efforts to get his work published. As soon as he received the two installments of *Pym* that had been published in the *Messenger*, Poe took them directly to Harper and Brothers. Following up on their original encouragement of Poe's efforts to write a novel, they accepted it, and in May the publisher issued an advance notice of its coming release.

But Poe's hopes for improving his finances with *Pym* soon collided with harsh reality. The week after Harper's announcement, a severe economic downturn struck the United States. In the ensuing Panic of 1837 the shortage of money that could be used for putting out new books caused Harper to delay publication of *Pym*. Just as serious for Poe, the poor state of the economy meant that the publishing companies and newspapers that might have hired Poe were unable to do so.

Nevertheless, Poe made good use of his time. He put in regular hours at home working with the editors and proofreaders from Harper, preparing for the day

BOARDINGHOUSE IN NEW YORK CITY

The bookseller William Gowans, whose account of the time he boarded with the Poes in New York City appears in The Poe Log, *edited by Dwight Thomas and David K. Jackson, found Poe a most agreeable person to be around.*

"For eight months or more, one house contained us, one table fed! During that time I saw much of him [Poe] and had an opportunity of conversing with him often, and I must say I never saw him the least affected with liquor, nor even descend to any known vice, while he was one of the most courteous, gentlemanly, and intelligent companions I have met with during my journeyings and haltings through divers divisions of the globe; besides, he had an extra inducement to be a good man as well as a good husband, for he had a wife of matchless beauty and loveliness. . . . Poe had a remarkably pleasing and prepossessing countenance, what the ladies would call decidedly handsome."

Pym could be published. Poe was also able to land an occasional assignment as a freelance writer. He wrote and sold to the *New York Review* a critique of John L. Stephens's *Incidents of Travel in Egypt, Arabia Petraea, and the Holy Land,* and he sold to the *Baltimore Book* of 1839 a short story titled "Siope—A Fable."

Yet success in financial terms remained elusive. By the end of 1837, Poe was thinking of other ways he might support himself and his little family.

4 "Coining One's Brain to Silver"

As 1838 opened, Poe was discouraged enough with the income his writing was generating to think of quitting the literary life. What convinced him not to quit is unclear, but Poe decided to give writing one more try.

MOVE TO PHILADELPHIA

This time Philadelphia, the home of the publishers Lea and Blanchard (formerly Lea and Carey), seemed a compatible location to put his talents to use. He was familiar with the Philadelphia papers, the *Saturday Courier* and *Godey's Lady's Book,* and he had other contacts, such as William Duane, who had been a contributor to the *Southern Literary Messenger,* and James Peddar, an English writer he met through the bookseller Gowans.

While making the rounds of newspapers and magazines in the city, Poe was brought to the attention of Thomas Wyatt, a scientist who was teaching in the Philadelphia schools. Wyatt hired Poe to edit two schoolbooks—one on shelled animals entitled *The Conchologist's First Book,* and the other *A Synopsis of Natural History.* Working on these projects brought in a little money, though not enough to support Poe, his wife, and his aunt.

BURTON'S GENTLEMAN'S MAGAZINE

Actually, working as a freelance writer was not what Poe really hoped to do in Philadelphia. Instead, he had begun to work out the editorial policies for what he planned would be his own literary magazine, which he called the *Penn.*

Poe knew, however, that such a project could not bring in money right away. Fortunately for his family, he also took advantage of his growing reputation as a writer and submitted some of his work to the recently established literary journal, *Burton's Gentleman's Magazine.*

It was not long before Poe also decided to approach the magazine's publisher, William Evans Burton, proposing that he be allowed to take on a few editorial responsibilities. In response, Burton offered to pay Poe ten dollars a week for working two hours a day at the magazine. Burton also promised to pay Poe for any of his own writing that the magazine published.

Poe's work at *Burton's* went well for several weeks. His editorial duties gradually expanded, so much so that the July 1839 issue listed him as the magazine's editor. The arrangement suited Poe at first, but it soon turned out to benefit Burton more than it did Poe. Although three of Poe's poems were published immediately, the money paid for his original work was deducted from his meager salary. Worse, from Poe's perspective, this effort on behalf of *Burton's* took up time he had wanted to spend on developing the *Penn*.

The same month that Poe made his debut as *Burton's* editor, Harper finally released *The Narrative of Arthur Gordon Pym*, although as planned Poe was not listed as the author. Instead, the preface stated that the late Arthur Gordon Pym had written the book with E. A. Poe's assistance. As had been true of his previous books, *Pym* sold poorly.

Godey's Lady's Book, *which published this illustration in 1843, was one of several Philadelphia publications with which Poe was familiar.*

The reviews of the book did little to enhance Poe's standing as an author. During July and August, among two dozen notices and reviews, only one, by New York editor Horace Greeley, was favorable. American reviewers generally found Pym's adventures hard to believe. Mostly, the reviewers debated who the actual author of the book might be.

A FAMOUS STORY

Meantime, Poe continued working on his fiction. A Baltimore-based magazine called the *American Museum* in its first issue published "Ligeia," which Poe later considered his best tale, and in September 1839 *Burton's* published "The Fall of the House of Usher." Unlike *Pym*, these stories seemed believable to their readers. Their immediate popularity encouraged Poe in what would become a trademark literary technique: recounting fantastic and impossible events in such a realistic fashion that the unbelievable came to seem real.

Poe's success took some by surprise. T. H. White, whose *Southern Literary Messenger* was still going strong, had rejected "The Fall of the House of Usher" in the belief that its content would not appeal to American readers. White had instructed his editorial assistant, James Heath, to write, "I doubt very much whether tales of the wild, improbable, and terrible class can ever be permanently popular in this country."[42] Even Poe's cousin Neilson, who was at the time working for the *Baltimore Chronicle,* had refused to publish a good word about the story.

In some ways "The Fall of the House of Usher" was familiar fare to its readers. In its setting it was similar to a much longer tale of supernatural horror by the German romantic writer Thomas H. Hoffman. Poe's original contribution was the emphasis he placed on both the narrator's and Roderick Usher's realistic and direct experience of the doomed family mansion.

"The Fall of the House of Usher" exemplifies Poe's ideal of composition—unity of effect. In later years, it was such unity that was credited with lending the tale its power to grip the imagination. Poe's nineteenth-century biographer George E. Woodberry says, "[I]t does not come short of absolute perfection. The adaptation of the related parts and their union in the total effect are a triumph of literary craft; the intricate details, as it were mellowing and reflecting one ground tone, have the definiteness and precision of inlaid mosaic."[43]

TALES OF THE GROTESQUE AND ARABESQUE

Thanks to the success of his stories, Poe was now more likely to find a buyer for his individual works and was receiving encouragement from other authors. The famous short-story writer Washington Irving wrote Poe, congratulating him for the success of "The Fall of the House of Usher."

But with Poe it remained important to have whole books to his credit. He would not give up the idea that his career depended on book publication rather than on the appearance of his shorter works in magazines. With the letter from Irving in hand, Poe approached Lea and Blanchard in Philadelphia and convinced them to reprint in book form the twenty-three stories he had so far published, plus another called "Why the Little Frenchman Wears His Hand in a Sling." Lea agreed to put out the two-volume collection, *Tales of the Grotesque and Arabesque,* so long as Poe gave up all claim to any profit the books might make and satisfied himself with a few complimentary copies for his personal distribution.

This illustration depicts a scene in Poe's story "The Fall of the House of Usher."

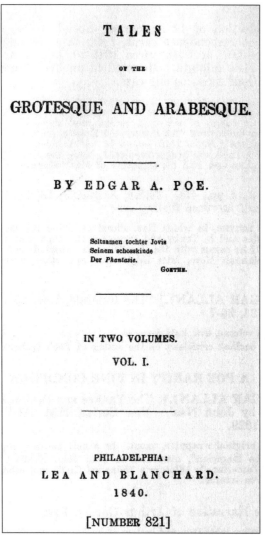

TALES

OF THE

GROTESQUE AND ARABESQUE.

BY EDGAR A. POE.

Seltsamen tochter Jovis
Seinem schosskinde
Der *Phantasie.*
GOETHE.

IN TWO VOLUMES.

VOL. I.

PHILADELPHIA:
LEA AND BLANCHARD.
1840.

[NUMBER 821]

The title page from Poe's first book of fiction, Tales of the Grotesque and Arabesque.

Published on December 4, 1839, *Tales of the Grotesque and Arabesque* represented the first eight years of Poe's fiction writing. The 750 copies Lea and Blanchard printed sold, though slowly, and the books received good reviews.

In spite of the positive reviews the collection received, however, Lea and Blan-

chard were dissatisfied with the advance sales of the book and wrote uncomplimentarily to Poe, on November 30, 1839, "when we undertook the *Tales'* publication, it was solely to oblige you and not with any view to profit. . . . If the offer to publish was now before us we should certainly decline it."[44]

Despite the lackluster sales at the time, Poe's biographer, James A. Harrison, comments that the stories reveal

> all the Poe types . . . in statuesque perfection: the lonely forlorn woman stricken with early disease and death; the tale of terror and conscience; the old-world romance; . . . the story whose germ is found in an exquisite poem imbedded in the text; . . . the wonderful fictions of pseudoscience; . . . the eloquent Platonic dialogue; . . . the humorous grotesque; . . . life-and-death with its dramatic self-realization. . . . To have accomplished all this . . . was to achieve a high and noble distinction.[45]

CONTINUED HOPES FOR THE *PENN*

Meanwhile, Poe was continuing to work at *Burton's,* but just as he had chafed under restrictions at the *Southern Literary Messenger,* he began to resent the supervision of Burton. Tensions between Poe and Burton mounted during the last weeks of May 1840, especially when Burton tried to tell Poe how far he could go with giving his opinion in reviews and how weird his stories could be.

At the same time, Poe was putting his hopes in his yet-to-be-launched magazine, the *Penn*, and was cautiously leaking the news of his plans to others in the American literary community. As word of Poe's project spread, some of his colleagues showed genuine enthusiasm. The New York–based editor of *Knickerbocker*, Lewis Gaylord Clark, wrote on June 4, in a letter to the poet Henry Wadsworth Longfellow, "We shall be pleased to find him reigning in his own sphere, where his classic power and genuine good taste, untrammeled by base or palsying association, shall have full scope and play. We do not doubt that the *Penn Magazine* will add to the reputation of its conductor and do honor to its name."[46]

As Poe's determination to launch the *Penn* gained strength, he left his job as editor in June 1840, and occupied his time with sending out his prospectus for the journal, asking everyone he knew to subscribe in advance. In letters he sent with

---

POE'S INCOME

After Poe resigned as editor of Burton's Gentleman's Magazine, *he wrote to William E. Burton about his pay. Poe's letter, included in* The Letters of Edgar Allan Poe, *edited by John Ward Ostrom, suggests that Burton got his money's worth from his former employee.*

"Soon after I joined you, you made me an offer of money, and I accepted $20. Upon another occasion, at my request, you sent me enclosed in a letter $30. Of this 30 I repaid 20 within the next fortnight (drawing no salary for that period). I was thus still in your debt $30, when not long ago I again asked a loan of $30, which you promptly handed to me at your own house. Within the last three weeks, three dollars each week have been retained from my salary, an indignity which I have felt deeply but did not resent. You state the sum retained as $8, but this I believe is through a mistake of Mr. Morrell. My postage bill, at a guess, might be $9 or $10—and I therefore am indebted to you, upon the whole, in the amount of about $60. More than this sum I shall not pay. You state that you can no longer afford to pay $50 per month for 2 or 3 pp of MS [manuscript]. Your error here can be shown by reference to the Magazine. During my year with you I have written— . . . 132 pp. . . . Nothing is counted but *bona fide* composition. 11 pp. at $3 per p. would be $33 [per month], at the usual Magazine prices. Deduct this from $50, my monthly salary, and we have left $17 per month, or $4.25 per week, for the services of proofreading; general superintendence at the printing office; reading, alteration, and preparation of MSS. . . . Upon the whole I am not willing to admit that you have greatly overpaid me."

his prospectus, Poe implied that editorial independence was his motivation for starting his own magazine. For example, in his letter to his cousin, William Poe, he was scathing in his criticism of his former employer T. H. White and simply ignored Burton altogether:

> Herewith I send you a Prospectus of my contemplated Magazine. I believe you know that my connection with the *Southern Messenger* was merely that of editor. I had no proprietary interest in it, and my movements were therefore much impeded. The situation was disagreeable to me in every respect. The drudgery was excessive; the salary was contemptible. In fact I soon found that whatever reputation I might personally gain, this reputation would be all. I stood no chance of bettering my pecuniary [financial] condition, while my best energies were wasted in the service of an illiterate and vulgar, although well-meaning man, who had neither the capacity to appreciate my labors, nor the will to reward them.[47]

ANOTHER SETBACK

In Poe's correspondence from June to November 1840 he consistently stated that the date for his first issue would be January 1841. Soliciting manuscripts and promising a quality magazine, he had considerable success in attracting both subscriptions and submissions of essays, poems, and stories. But the end of the year brought a new concern that interrupted his plans to get the

Penn started. In October Poe became involved in the heated presidential campaign of 1840 between William Henry Harrison and Martin Van Buren.

The result of Poe's dabbling in politics was that on December 30, 1840, he was forced to write to his subscribers and contributors to tell them, as he wrote to one contributor named L. J. Cist, "[a] severe illness . . . has confined me to bed for the last month . . . from which I am now only slowly recovering. The worse result of this illness is that I am forced to postpone the issue of the first number of the Mag. until the first of March next."[48]

The illness Poe referred to was likely due in part to alcohol consumption, says biog-

Poe's involvement in the presidential campaign of William Henry Harrison (pictured) delayed publication of the first issue of the Penn.

POE'S CAT

Catterina, the family cat, had a secure place in Poe's home, apparently earning his respect for her intelligence, as is shown in this excerpt from his article "Instinct Versus Reason," included in Collected Works of Edgar Allan Poe: Tales and Sketches, *edited by Thomas Ollive Mabbot.*

"The writer of this article is the owner of one of the most remarkable black cats in the world—and this is saying much; for it will be remembered that black cats are all of them witches. The one in question has not a white hair about her, and is of a demure and sanctified demeanor. That portion of the kitchen which she frequents is accessible only by a door, which closes with what is termed a thumb-latch; these latches are rude in construction, and some force and dexterity are always requisite to force them down. But puss is in the daily habit of opening the door, which she accomplishes in the following way. She first springs from the ground to the guard of the latch (which resembles the guard over a gun-trigger), and through this she thrusts her left arm to hold on with. She now, with her right hand, presses the thumb-latch until it yields, and here several attempts are frequently requisite. Having forced it down, however, she seems to be aware that her task is but half accomplished, since, if the door is not pushed open before she lets go, the latch will again fall into its socket. She, therefore, screws her body round so as to bring her hind feet immediately beneath the latch, while she leaps with all her strength from the door—the impetus of the spring forcing it open, and her hind feet sustaining the latch until this impetus is fairly given.

We have witnessed this singular feat a hundred times at least, and never without being impressed with the truth of the remark with which we commenced this article—that the boundary between instinct and reason is of a very shadowy nature."

rapher William Bittner. In his commentary on this letter, Bittner states that the pressure of the political campaign motivated Poe to drink excessively. Around election time,

Bittner says, Poe had "surrendered to the availability of the barrel of hard cider. This, compounded with his hard work and the tensions of attempting to found a magazine without capital and to support his family without an income, caused him to be struck down with illness."[49]

ANOTHER REASON TO POSTPONE THE *PENN*

Burton, meanwhile, had continued to publish *Burton's Gentleman's Magazine,* although he was losing interest in the venture himself. By the time Poe's subscribers were learning of the postponement of the *Penn,* Burton was negotiating the sale of his publication to George Rex Graham, then owner and editor of a journal entitled *Atkinson's Casket,* also based in Philadelphia.

As he closed the sale of his magazine, Burton did Poe one last favor. In spite of Poe's having resigned weeks earlier, Burton said to Graham, "There is one thing more: I want you to take care of my young editor."[50]

Graham did not immediately act upon Burton's request. But as Poe continued into March with efforts to sell his writing, Graham inquired about the *Penn.* Upon learning directly from Poe of the postponement of the magazine's launch, Graham proposed that at the end of six months he and Poe might go into partnership on that venture. In the interim, Graham suggested, Poe should be acting editor of what would be called *Graham's Magazine.*

A BIGGER JOB

Being editor of *Graham's Magazine* became the new engine that drove Poe's career, as he quickly became one of the publication's major contributors of articles and stories. In keeping with Poe's ability to turn personal experience into magazine fare, the first issues carried his two political satires "Peter Pendulum, the Business Man" and "Never Bet Your Head."

This was a time of relative ease in Poe's life. Now receiving a little higher salary, eight hundred dollars a year, Poe moved his family to a house on Coates Street, bought a few pieces of furniture and purchased a harp for Virginia. He went for walks and on hunting forays and enjoyed the beauty of his eighteen-year-old wife.

Still, at the conclusion of Poe's first six months as *Graham's Magazine* editor, his finances were such that plans for the *Penn* remained in limbo. The American economy was continuing to do poorly, which meant that there were few subscribers and thus inadequate money for Poe to get his cherished project off the ground. Moreover, virtually all Poe's time was devoted to writing for *Graham's Magazine.*

POE'S WRITING CAREER

Faced with the need for more and more copy for *Graham's Magazine,* there was almost nothing that he produced that Poe did not use in some way. Reflecting on his experiences, for example, he showed his love of walking through the woods in his nature sketch, "Morning on the Wissahiccon."

Other personalized works drew either on childhood memories or on the pleasure he was finding in his marriage to Virginia. His story "Eleanora" celebrates the love of husband and wife. His short story "Man of the Crowd" contained descriptions he remembered from his stay in London as a child and goes on to reveal a struggle with conscience over greed.

In his critiques of the works of others Poe often took the opportunity to launch his own ideas, while relating them to ideas in the books he was reviewing. For exam-ple, while he was writing his review of a book by Lambert A. Wilmer, *The Quacks of Helicon*, Poe explained in a letter that he was using "the text . . . to preach a fire-&-fury sermon upon critical independence, and the general literary humbuggery of the day."[51]

No topic was too offbeat to find its way into Poe's writing. For example, he of-fered to solve cryptograms—messages

This engraving of Poe reflects his interest in fanciful subject matter.

written in code—for anyone who sent them in. The results of his challenge occupied many hours of his time. He presented to the American public one of the first promotions of photography, explaining the process of the daguerreotype, first demonstrated in Paris only weeks before his article appeared in 1841. After becoming interested in phrenology (studying the shape of the skull to somehow discern a person's character), he analyzed his own and others' personalities in this way.

LIFELONG ASSOCIATES

Poe's work at *Graham's Magazine,* meanwhile, rewarded him in an intangible way. While he worked there, Poe spent time with writers and publishers who would be influential throughout the rest of his life. Foremost among those was the novelist Frederick William Thomas, author of *Clinton Bradshaw* and *Howard Pinckney.*

Poe had first become acquainted with Thomas and his family when he was living in Baltimore, and the two men now struck up a correspondence. Thomas also happened to be friends with the U.S. president, John Tyler, and had obtained a political appointment in Tyler's administration because of that friendship.

Seeing his friend find a job through political influence captured Poe's imagination. Concluding that a government job would suit his own needs, Poe asked Thomas to approach the president and his son, Robert Tyler, regarding an appointment for Poe. "I would be glad," Poe wrote on July 4, 1841, "to get almost any

appointment—even a $500 one—so that I have something independent of letters for a subsistence. To coin one's brain into silver, at the nod of a master, is to my thinking the hardest task in the world."[52]

THE FIRST MODERN DETECTIVE STORY

Poe continued, however, to coin his brain into silver at *Graham's Magazine* and to receive better and better responses from its readers. Although he secretly hoped for the Tyler administration to come across with a government job for him, he could not help but rejoice that his literary fame was spreading.

"The Murders in the Rue Morgue," published in April 1841, was one tale that received compliments from critics and friends alike. In this story, a French investigator named Dupin uses reasoning and analysis to discover that a killer ape has committed crimes the police could not solve. The use of logic—what Poe called ratiocination—to solve a crime was new in the literature of the day and was directly opposed to the intuitive or emotional appeal other writers were using in their works.

Another friend and critic, Joseph Evans Snodgrass, was particularly complimentary of Poe's effort. Poe thanked Snodgrass for his compliments on his story and agreed with him that "The Murders in the Rue Morgue" was one of his better pieces. But even as he appreciated the compliments, Poe downplayed the originality of the tale and the difficulty of writing it, as

This illustration depicts a scene from Poe's "The Murders in the Rue Morgue," which many scholars consider the first modern detective story.

he explained in detail to his poet friend Philip E. Cooke:

> You are right about the hair-splitting of my French friend:—that is all done for effect. These tales of ratiocination owe most of their popularity to being something in a new key. I do not mean to say that they are not ingenious—but people think them more ingenious than they are—on account of their method and air of method. In

the "Murders in the Rue Morgue," for instance, where is the ingenuity of unravelling a web which you yourself have woven for the express purpose of unravelling? The reader is made to confound the ingenuity of the supposititious Dupin with that of the writer of the story.[53]

THE SECOND AMERICAN DETECTIVE STORY

Poe followed up the success of "The Murders of the Rue Morgue" with a sequel, "The Mystery of Marie Roget." In this letter, which is reproduced in The Letters of Edgar Allan Poe, *edited by John Ward Ostrom, he suggests that his story and the investigative techniques his character, Dupin, uses will be of value in the investigation of an actual murder case in New York City.*

"I have just completed . . . 'The Mystery of Marie Roget—a Sequel to the Murders in the Rue Morgue.' The story is based upon the assassination of Mary Cecilia Rogers, which created so vast an excitement, some months ago, in New York. I have, however, handled my design in a manner altogether *novel* in literature. I have imagined a series of nearly exact *coincidences* occurring in Paris. A young *grisette* [clerk], one Marie Roget, has been murdered under precisely similar circumstances with Mary Rogers. Thus, under pretence of showing how Dupin [the hero of 'The Rue Morgue'] unravelled the mystery of Marie's assassination, I, in reality, enter into a very long and rigorous analysis of the New York tragedy. No point is omitted. I examine, each by each, the opinions and arguments of the press upon the subject, and show that this subject has been, hitherto, *unapproached*. In fact, I believe not only that I have demonstrated the fallacy of the general idea—that the girl was the victim of a gang of ruffians—but have *indicated the assassin* in a manner which will give renewed impetus to investigation. My main object, nevertheless, as you will readily understand, is an analysis of the true principles which should direct inquiry in similar cases. From the nature of the subject, I feel convinced that the article will excite attention, and it has occurred to me that you would be willing to purchase it for the forthcoming *Mammoth Notion*. It will make 25 pages in *Graham's Magazine;* and, at the usual price, would be worth to me $100. For reasons, however, which I need not specify, I am desirous of having this tale printed in Boston, and, if you like it, I will say $50."

Thanks to the success of his fiction, 1841 was a time of financial promise for Poe as well as benefit for *Graham's Magazine*. Biographer John H. Ingram writes:

[Graham] speedily received due reward for his appreciation of Poe's talents. Indeed, it is declared that in a little less than two years the number of subscribers to the magazine increased from five to fifty-two thousand, and this, although aided by Mr. Graham's liberality to his contributors, was mainly due to the new editor. His daring critiques, his analytic essays, and his weird stories, following one another in rapid succession, startled the public and compelled it to an acknowledgement of his powers.[54]

Yet troubled times lay ahead for Poe and his family.

5 Tragedy Strikes and Stays

As 1842 opened, Poe was enjoying both fame and good fortune. His family was comfortably situated, and he was bringing in a steady, if small, income. Hervey Allen in his biography, *Israfel,* describes that time in idyllic terms:

> [T]here never was a time in his life when there were so few clouds visible on the horizon; when his prospects appeared so bright. . . . He was, apparently for him, fairly well; and, for the time being, he braced himself to meet the responsibilities of a new position by letting [alcohol] alone. He was the respected and feared editor and critic of an important, if not the most important, magazine in the country. Although comparatively poor, his home was comfortable and even pretty. Virginia . . . was still able to accompany him on Sunday rambles or picnics up the Wissahiccon [River]. Above all he was growing in fame, and, for the time being, seemed surrounded by friends old and new. These delighted to gather at the Coates Street house, kept spotless by Mrs. Clemm, who managed Poe's bank account carefully. She and Virginia added all they could by taking in sewing.[55]

Then Poe's comfort and pleasure with his home life suddenly collapsed. One evening in late January 1842, a small group had gathered for a pleasant evening of Poe hospitality with Virginia singing and playing the harp. Biographer Hervey Allen relates what happened:

> The girl-wife with the large bright eyes and the waxen face ran her childish hands over the wires and began to sing. There was something peculiarly angelic and ethereal about this sight of Virginia playing the harp in the parlor by her own fireside that almost transported Poe. . . . The notes mounted higher, very true and clear—suddenly she stopped, clutched her throat, and a wave of crimson rushed down over her breast. Poe— all of them sprang to her. For a while it seemed certain that she must die. Stained with her life blood, he carried her upstairs and laid her on the bed.[56]

The doctor was fetched, and Virginia survived the immediate crisis, but their life changed dramatically. Now Poe seemed obsessed with the certainty that he would lose his lovely young wife to tuberculosis, the same disease that had taken so many other loved ones from him.

POE LEAVES *GRAHAM'S MAGAZINE*

For several weeks Poe divided his attention among his editorial duties, his care for Virginia, and work on his poetry and fiction. He published three more tales and three poems in *Graham's Magazine*. Thanks to his reputation, the publication was thriving. The printers were now issuing forty thousand copies of each issue. The popularity of *Graham's Magazine* did not, however, translate into plenty for Poe. He was being paid so little that often the only food the family could afford was bread and molasses. They sold their furniture to bring in money for basic necessities.

Poe found some solace in his work, but there was always the specter of Virginia's illness. Hervey Allen writes,

> It was a life of enormous, absurd, and grotesquely tragic contrasts. There

Poe, pictured here, became obsessed about the possibility of losing his wife to tuberculosis, the same disease that had killed his mother.

would be an afternoon spent idly with [Poe's friend] Henry Hirst talking poetry. . . . The night would be spent with Virginia, trying to stop her terrible choking. He would walk the floor with her, the tell-tale red spots on his shirt bosom next morning driving him half insane.[57]

Still, Poe persisted, not only in producing new works but in finding new ways to make what he had already produced pay off for him. For example, when Poe learned that the English novelist Charles Dickens was coming to America in early 1842 and that one of his stops was to be the office of *Graham's Magazine,* he wrote to Dickens, asking for an appointment to see the famous author. Dickens, Poe hoped, could help him get his work published in Britain.

The two writers met on March 7. Before Dickens left Philadelphia, Poe had convinced him to look for an English publisher to reprint *Tales of the Grotesque and Arabesque.* Poe also found Dickens was sympathetic to his concern that writers in both the United States and Britain should be protected from unscrupulous printers who made a practice of pirating work from the other side of the Atlantic. Despite the apparent cordiality, however, Dickens did not follow through on his promise of help, either with British publication of *Tales* or with work on copyright protection.

Poe's work at *Graham's Magazine* was made more difficult because he was so often kept up late caring for Virginia. Often tired during the day, Poe fell behind in his work. To ease Poe's load, Graham hired a part-time helper, a onetime clergyman named Rufus Wilmot Griswold.

Poe accepted the help for a while, but he soon felt his job was threatened by Griswold's constant presence. Poe's concern proved well founded. As his biographer Hervey Allen tells it, "One day in April, when Poe came to the office after an absence, he found the Reverend Griswold occupying the editorial chair. Poe took the situation in at a glance, turned on his heel and never entered the place again."[58]

Poe officially left *Graham's Magazine* in May although he remained on good terms with its owner. But Poe's replacement by Griswold was the beginning of years of professional jealousy and personal enmity. The two disagreed on almost every literary and moral issue and exchanged numerous public criticisms of each other's opinions and actions.

Poe put a good face on leaving the magazine, saying he needed more time to gather subscriptions for the *Penn* and to write many letters to promote it, but his protestations did not change the fact that Poe was nearly starving. "The Mystery of Marie Roget," a sequel to "The Murders in the Rue Morgue," brought in a little money, but his hopes of financial independence kept him pursuing a government job. In May, he wrote to Frederick W. Thomas, now living in Washington, D.C., "It would relieve me of all care as regards a mere subsistence, and thus allow me time for thought, which, in fact, is action."[59]

A Distressing Time

At the same time, his wife's illness was constantly on his mind, and some of the stories from this time reflect Poe's distress.

GRISWOLD, POE'S ENEMY

Hervey Allen, in Israfel, *writes of how the Reverend Rufus Wilmot Griswold gained access to detailed information about Poe's personal life, which he later used against his literary opponent when he wrote his biography of Poe.*

"There can be no doubt that it was in Philadelphia, during the Spring and Summer of 1843, that Griswold became unhappily familiar with the presence of Mrs. Clemm, who was frequently at that time forced to carry Edgar's manuscripts to *Graham's,* or the offices of other publications, and to call upon the editors to dun them for payment or advances while playing upon their sympathy. Through Mrs. Clemm, Griswold and others became privy to the inmost troubles of the Poe household and the shadows of its tragedy. That Griswold used this information to strike with a concealed hand against Poe, and that he afterward exploited Mrs. Clemm in her dire poverty, while at the same time realizing [his revenge] upon the writings of his dead friend [Poe] and damning his reputation, is a proven fact which must be remembered when taking his evidence."

During Poe's absence from Graham's *to care for his ailing wife, the Reverend Rufus Griswold took Poe's job and the men became lifelong enemies as a result.*

Among them were "The Pit and the Pendulum," a story of terror and unmotivated torture; "The Black Cat," about a man's terrible remorse over torturing and killing his beloved cat; as well as "Life in Death" and "The Masque of the Red Death." In fact, writes Bittner, during his last weeks at *Graham's Magazine,*

> [Poe] was well into completing a good stock of stories of a strange, morbid sort, . . . "Life in Death" (later called "The Oval Portrait") . . . is the account of a sickly traveler who . . . is entranced by a strangely lifelike portrait of a young

woman. He looked into a catalogue of paintings and there learned that it was a painting of the artist's wife, who had sickened and died while sitting for it, seemingly as if life had passed from her to the picture. This he wrote in expiation of the extent to which Virginia's illness had been aggravated by the poverty they had suffered through Poe's dedication to his art.

Far more gruesomely autobiographical, however, was the symbolic fantasy of color which he called "The Masque of the Red Death," . . . [in which] Prince

It was during his wife's illness that Poe penned a number of gruesome and horrific tales, including "The Masque of the Red Death," a scene from which is depicted here.

Prospero and a thousand friends take refuge in a walled abbey to escape the "Red Death," a plague of "sharp pains, and sudden dizziness, and then profuse bleeding at the pores, with dissolution."[60]

DESPERATE SOLICITATIONS FOR A GOVERNMENT JOB

Now that Poe was no longer drawing a salary, the family found it necessary to move to less expensive quarters. They found a rundown three-story brick house near Spring Garden Street, farther out from the center of town. Its large pear tree and flower garden were a pleasant refuge for Poe, his wife, and his aunt.

Virginia's health was poor, but she was still able to receive visitors. Poe's colleagues, as well as relatives and friends came to call, including people from as far away as Baltimore and Richmond. "The neighbors and their children, in love with Virginia, were much in and out," writes Allen. "Even Rufus Griswold came to see, and was softened, almost to tenderness, in spite of himself."[61]

Faced with the unrelenting needs of his family and the lack of income from his writing, Poe devoted still more attention to getting a job working for the government. To those who might be influential he spoke again and again of a position in the Philadelphia customs house, something that would be a source of steady income and yet allow him the time to work on building support for his literary maga-

zine, which he now referred to by its new name, the *Stylus*.

The prospects for obtaining some kind of government appointment looked good. For one thing, Poe's friend Frederick W. Thomas was living in Washington, with close access to President Tyler and his son. Both Thomas and Poe were on friendly terms with J. P. Kennedy, who was well connected in Washington. Poe even fantasized that his short stay at West Point might somehow help in getting him an appointment.

But several months passed, and by August Poe was nearly frantic, begging Thomas for news of progress in getting word to President Tyler of his needs. He even considered going back to his old job at *Graham's Magazine*, telling Thomas that "Graham has made me a good offer to return. He is not especially pleased with Griswold—nor is anyone else, with the exception of the Rev. gentleman himself." Yet Poe held off, for he still felt hopeful that his friend might be able to help. He noted that he was "happy to say that Virginia's health has slightly improved. My spirits are proportionately good. Perhaps all will yet go well."[62]

Thomas, however, became so concerned over how the delay in obtaining Poe's appointment was affecting his friend's mental state that he visited Poe's home in September. That visit made the need for action seem even more pressing. It appeared to him that Poe had been drinking, since he found him still in bed at a time when most people would have long since been up and around:

Although I arrived late in the morning Mrs. Clemm, Poe's mother-in-law, was busy preparing for his breakfast.

My presence possibly caused some confusion, but I noticed that there was delay and evident difficulty in procuring the meal. His wife entertained me. Her manners were agreeable and graceful. She had well formed, regular features, with the most expressive and intelligent eyes I have ever beheld. Her pale complexion, the deep lines in her face and a consumptive cough made me regard her as the victim for an early grave. She and her mother showed much concern about Eddie, as they called Poe, and were anxious to have him secure work. I afterwards learned from Poe that he had been to New York in search of employment and had also made effort to get out an edition of his tales, but was unsuccessful.[63]

Whether Poe had in fact been drinking on that occasion is unclear, but he agreed to accept treatment for alcoholism. Thomas helped arrange for his friend to spend a week at the fashionable spa at Saratoga Springs, Virginia, and Poe swore once again that he would give up alcohol.

DREAMING ON ABOUT THE STYLUS

No appointment had come by the end of the year, and Poe vacillated between hope for a government job and hope that the long-delayed *Stylus* would finally become a reality. The *Stylus,* in Poe's mind at least, continued to take shape. He told a prospective supporter, Dr. Thomas Holley Chivers, about the size of the magazine and the expenses he anticipated. In a letter to the poet James Russell Lowell, Poe indicated that he was now planning the first issue for July 1843.

Meanwhile, Poe kept busy at other chores. He had become closely associated with the Philadelphia *Saturday Museum* and his old nemesis Griswold hired him to write for it a review of his anthology, *Poets and Poetry of America.* The article Poe wrote, however, was severely critical of Griswold's volume. Because the volume was meant to make a profit, Poe charged, Griswold was accepting poor poems in hopes that his contributors would buy the ornate annual. As a result of this review, Griswold's hatred of Poe only grew more intense.

THE ONLY FEARLESS AMERICAN CRITIC

Not only was Poe's campaign for a government job stalled, but once again, plans for the *Stylus* had to be put off. One of Poe's and Thomas's friends, Thomas Clarke, had agreed to contribute money to the project, but deciding that the financial climate in the nation was still too unreliable to allow a magazine to survive, he withdrew his support. Clarke's decision seemed only prudent in light of subsequent events. James Russell Lowell had founded a magazine in Boston, called the *Pioneer,* but after only two months he was forced to discontinue publication.

The demise of the *Pioneer* hurt Poe both directly and indirectly. Lowell had been one of Poe's strongest advocates, calling

James Russell Lowell was one of Poe's strongest advocates and the failure of Lowell's magazine, the Pioneer, *was a blow for Poe.*

him "almost the only *fearless* American critic."[64] Worse, perhaps, for Poe, Lowell had published Poe's tale "The Tell-Tale Heart" but when his magazine failed, he was unable even to pay Poe the ten dollars he had promised him for his story.

With no government appointment and his writing failing to provide income, there was almost no money in the Poe house. Mrs. Clemm was taking in boarders, and she also was contributing by sewing for others. But again and again Poe was forced to beg friends and acquaintances for loans, even Rufus Griswold.

George Graham continued to be friendly. In January 1843, he paid Poe the going price for his poem "The Conqueror Worm." Scholars see in this poem's imagery strong allusions to Virginia's tuberculosis and its attendant hemorrhaging, especially in the words: "A blood-red thing that writhes from out / The scenic solitude! / It writhes!—it writhes!—with mortal pangs / The mimes become its food."[65]

GEORGE GRAHAM PRAISES POE

George Rex Graham, Poe's colleague, employer, and friend, owner of Graham's Magazine, *wrote this assessment of Poe's life and character on February 2, 1850, after seeing Rufus W. Griswold's damning biography of Poe. It is included in* The Works of Edgar Allan Poe *published in 1876 by Armstrong & Son.*

"The very natural question—'Why did he not work and thrive?' is easily answered. It will not be asked by the many who know the precarious tenure by which literary men hold a mere living in this country. The avenues through which they can profitably reach the country are few, and crowded with aspirants for bread as well as fame. The unfortunate tendency to cheapen every literary work to the lowest point of beggarly flimsiness in price and profit, prevents even the well-disposed from extending anything like an adequate support to even a part of the great throng which genius, talent, education and even misfortune, force into struggle. The character of Poe's mind was of such an order as not to be very widely in demand. The class of educated mind which he could readily and profitably address was small—the channels through which he could do so at all were few—and publishers all, or nearly all, contented with such pens as were already engaged, hesitated to incur the expense of his to an extent which would sufficiently remunerate him."

Graham also proposed publishing Poe's stories in a series of pamphlets titled *The Prose Romances of Edgar Allan Poe.* The first volume was published, but its sales were poor. As a result, Graham scrapped his plans for future pamphlets. This small paperback, however, received favorable notices, which ultimately were key to winning Poe a broader readership.

Some of Poe's writing did earn money, although never enough to pull the family out of poverty. He won a one-hundred-dollar prize for another mystery story, "The Gold Bug." As with "The Murders in the Rue Morgue," this tale was one that involved the use of logic: the narrator cracks a code to uncover a hidden treasure. Poe drew on his memories from his days at Fort Moultrie, on Sullivan's Island, in creating the story's setting. The *Dollar Newspaper* published "The Gold Bug" in June 1843. Later, a special edition, illustrated by Felix O. C. Darley, one of the leading artists of the day, came out and went through several reprintings. "The Gold Bug" was significant in that it was Poe's first nationally popular story. So successful was this tale with readers that a play based on it was produced—the only Poe tale to receive that treatment during his lifetime.

On the Lecture Circuit

In addition to his writing, Poe had a few chances to bring in a little cash with lectures. These lectures were on a variety of literary topics, and often were designed to publicize Griswold's *Poets and Poetry of America,* but Poe also used them as a platform for publicizing his plans for the *Stylus.*

Poe also had hoped that one lecture would advance his hope of landing a government job. His friends Frederick Thomas and Thomas Clarke arranged for Poe to give his presentation at the White House. Unfortunately, the plan went awry. Before he went to the White House, Poe got drunk and spent all the money he had. He did get to see the president, but he was still not sober and so succeeded only in making a poor impression.

Poe returned home without giving his lecture. He asked Thomas to help repair the

The Philadelphia home where the Poe family lived from 1842 to 1844 is still standing today and is open to the public.

An Interest in Science: A History in Photographs

Poe was an avid reader, not just of literature but also of scientific works. For example, his interest in the discovery of the first practical photographic process in France resulted in an article, "The Daguerreotype," just six weeks later—January 15, 1840, in *Alexander's Weekly Messenger*. Almost as soon as shops where daguerreotypes were taken appeared in the United States, Poe sat for a portrait.

The process of daguerreotyping may explain Poe's strained expression in some of his likenesses, because sitting for a daguerreotype required its subject to remain motionless for several minutes in bright daylight, not even blinking, while a copper plate coated with silver-iodide was slowly exposed inside the camera.

Cameras like this one were used in the process of daguerreotyping, an invention of great interest to Edgar Allan Poe.

damage he had done, writing, "I would be glad, if you would take an opportunity of saying to Mr. Rob. Tyler that if he *can* look over matters & get me the Inspectorship, I will join the Washingtonians forthwith. I am as serious as a judge—& much more so than many."[66]

Poe tried to put the incident at the White House in a humorous light, noting, "I think it would be a feather in Mr. Tyler's cap to save from the perils of mint julip & port wines a young man of whom all the world thinks so well and who thinks so remarkably well of himself."[67] The upshot of Poe's performance was, however, that his hopes for a paying job with the government were at an end.

Following the trip to Washington, Poe went back to work on a freelance basis for papers in Philadelphia and New York as well as to solving cryptograms to earn a little cash.

Poe also continued giving lectures. Charging twenty-five cents per ticket for two successful lectures in Baltimore on *Poets and Poetry of America*, he directly attacked the work of Henry Wadsworth Longfellow, who, he said, used verse to make moralistic points. Since the purpose of poetry was solely to fashion works of beauty, Poe said, Longfellow was unworthy of the acclaim he received.

In spite of his attacks, or perhaps because of their controversial nature, Poe's lectures were well received. On January 31 and again on March 12, 1844, "he was greeted by a large audience and they testified their appreciation by repeated bursts of applause."[68] His friend Joseph Evans Snodgrass noted in the *Saturday*

Poe was highly critical of the works of Henry Wadsworth Longfellow, pictured here.

Visitor that his attacks were particularly hard on Griswold: "[Poe] was very entertaining, and enforced his views well—though to some of them we cannot assent. For instance—that the incultation of truth is not the highest aim of poetry! He was witheringly severe upon Rufus W. Griswold."[69]

Poe's six years in Philadelphia were assessed by his biographer Arthur Hobson Quinn as marking the top of his career as a man of letters. He had edited what at that time was considered the most prestigious magazine in the country. Through his publication of thirty-seven stories and a number of well-received poems, Quinn notes, "he had become widely known, and if he had made enemies, he also had made friends. For part of his stay in Philadelphia he was even happy, and when he left it, it is not too much to say that he left happiness behind."[70] Poe was restless, though, and prepared to move. Once more he decided to try his luck in New York City.

6 The Depths and the Heights

Poe decided that the only place where he could hope to find a better life was New York City. With eleven dollars in his pocket, he left Philadelphia on April 6, 1844, accompanied by Virginia. Mrs. Clemm stayed behind to sell off the few remaining pieces of furniture and was to join the couple in May, bringing Catterina, the family cat, with her.

The journey by boat and train brought the couple to lower Manhattan the next evening. Upon their arrival Poe immediately wrote to his aunt to allay her worries about Virginia and to describe the room he had rented at a boardinghouse for a dollar a day.

IMMEDIATE PUBLICATION

In New York, Poe lost no time in approaching Richard Adams Locke of the *Sun* with his story narrating an imaginary transatlantic balloon voyage. In his story, which was later entitled "The Balloon Hoax," Poe tells of a planned flight between London and Paris that goes awry when a freak air current takes the balloon across the ocean to the United States instead.

The *Sun* bought the story and ran it as though it were a legitimate news item, and Poe was delighted with the large number of people who bought the hoax. The idea had been to increase circulation for the paper and consequently to ensure that Locke would buy future stories, although that aspect of the plan never bore fruit. Several papers ran notices, comments, and reprints of this unsigned story.

INSPIRATION IN THE COUNTRY

Poe hoped to find inspiration for his work, and as part of his quest he often walked miles from his Greenwich Village boardinghouse and made contact with people living in the country. It was on one of his walks that he became acquainted with the owners of a two-hundred-acre vegetable farm on the outskirts of the city. This Irish couple, Mr. and Mrs. Patrick Brennan, were taken with Poe's charm and gave him a bargain on the rent for a house that was large enough to accommodate him, Virginia, and Maria Clemm.

A lady exits a stagecoach in Greenwich Village, New York. The Poe family made a Greenwich Village boardinghouse their new home in April 1844.

The rustic house provided Poe with a place to write and afforded the whole family with healthful surroundings. In this bucolic setting, poverty and tragedy seemed, for a while, not quite so close. The rural environment allowed Virginia and her mother to find fresh food. For Poe this was a peaceful place conducive to his creativity.

Poe had for some time been at work on a major poem, and in the old house, he found an image that he would use in this work, "The Raven." Over the door that opened from his study into the hallway was a shelf, and sitting on it was a small plaster head of Pallas Athena, the Greek goddess of wisdom. This image inspired Poe as he polished the poem he had determined would be his masterpiece.

Yet, even as he concentrated on "The Raven," Poe worked on other projects. In May he became a regular news correspondent providing articles about events in New York for the Philadelphia-based paper, *Columbia Spy*.

Poe also produced a number of other prose works in a remarkably short time.

ARRIVAL IN NEW YORK CITY

Poe's first letter to Maria Clemm from New York City reveals how far he could stretch the eleven dollars he had when he arrived from Philadelphia, as well as hinting at how sick his wife Virginia really was. It appears in Letters of Edgar Allan Poe, *edited by John Ward Ostrom.*

"Dear Muddie, . . .

Sissy [Virginia] coughed none at all. When we got to the wharf it was raining hard. I left her on board the boat, after putting the trunks in the Ladies' cabin, and set off to buy an umbrella and look for a boarding-house. I met a man selling umbrellas, and bought one for 62 cents. Then I went up Greenwich St. and soon found a boarding-house. It is just before you get to Cedar St., on the west side going up—the left-hand side. It has brown stone steps, with a porch with brown pillars. "Morrison" is the name on the door. I made a bargain in a few minutes and then got a hack and went for Sis. I was not gone more than $1/2$ an hour, and she was quite astonished to see me back so soon. She didn't expect me for an hour. There were 2 other ladies waiting on board—so she wasn't very lonely.—When we got to the house we had to wait about $1/2$ an hour before the room [was ready]. The house is old & looks buggy . . . but the landlady is a nice chatty old lady who gave us the back room on the night & day & attendance, for $7—the cheapest board I ever knew, taking into consideration the central situation and the *living*. I wish Kate [Catterina, the cat] could see it—she would faint. Last night, for supper, we had the nicest tea you ever drank, strong & hot—wheat & rye bread—cheese—tea-cakes (elegant), a great dish (2 dishes) of elegant ham, and 2 of cold veal, piled up like a mountain and large slices—3 dishes of the cakes and everything in the greatest profusion. No fear of starving here. The landlady seemed as if she couldn't press us enough, and we were at home directly. Her husband is living with her—a fat, good-natured old soul. there are eight or ten boarders—2 or 3 of them ladies—2 servants. For breakfast we had excellent-flavored coffee, hot and strong—not very clear & no great deal of cream—veal cutlets, elegant ham & eggs & nice bread and butter. I never sat down to a more plentiful or a nicer breakfast. I wish you could have seen the eggs—and the great dishes of meat. I ate the first hearty breakfast I have eaten since I left our little home. Sis is delighted, and we are both in excellent spirits. She has coughed hardly any and had no night sweat. She is now busy mending my pants which I tore against a nail. I went out last night and bought a skein of silk, a skein of thread, & 2 buttons, a pair of slippers, & a tin pan for the stove. The fire kept in all night. We have now got $4 and a half left."

Before December he had published two more of his weird stories: "The Oblong Box," about a grieving husband's attempt to preserve his wife's dead body, and "The Premature Burial," about a person buried alive in a coffin with an escape mechanism built into it. A sketch called "Desultory Notes on Cats" and a tale, "The Angel of the Odd," followed. In December the *Southern Literary Messenger* carried his satiric tale, "The Literary Life of Thingum Bob, ESQ."

A TIME-CONSUMING JOB

The writing of tales brought in enough for Poe to pay the rent regularly, but his aunt decided that he should have a regular job. In a move that friends saw as supporting Poe but critics have since characterized as domineering and meddlesome, Maria Clemm walked the five miles to the editorial office of Nathaniel Parker Willis, who was running two papers, the *New York Evening Mirror* and the *New York Weekly Mirror,* and convinced him to hire her nephew.

Thus Poe began once more to bring in a regular—if modest—salary working half days for Willis. His job was varied and entailed clipping items from other papers, writing reviews and advertisements, copy editing, helping with the papers' layout, and the myriad other chores involved in putting out a daily as well as a weekly paper.

Poe submitted to the boredom of performing these necessary tasks, and Willis considered him "a quiet, patient, industrious, and most gentlemanly person, commanding the utmost respect and good feelings by his unvarying deportment and ability."[71] From early October 1844 until early in 1845, Poe worked regularly at the *Mirror,* though he earned very little. In his free time he continued to work at finishing "The Raven."

In addition to polishing "The Raven," Poe worked at other projects. He wrote a review of Longfellow's anthology, *Waif,* for the *Mirror.* For *Godey's Lady's Book,* he wrote a story entitled "The Thousand-and-Second Tale of Scheherazade." The editors of the *American Review: A Whig Journal* scheduled his tale, "Some Words With a Mummy" for publication in April 1845.

A STEP UP IN THE EDITING WORLD

Meanwhile events were unfolding that appeared to be a step toward achieving Poe's dream of owning a literary journal. Poe had for some time maintained his correspondence with the poet James Russell Lowell. As 1844 drew to a close, their letters often concerned the biography of Poe that Lowell was writing for *Graham's Magazine.* When a friend of Lowell's, Charles F. Briggs, proposed starting a weekly magazine called the *Broadway Journal,* Lowell suggested that Poe would be a capable assistant and might even make a good third partner in the enterprise, along with John Bisco, who was providing the financing.

CLEMM'S INTERFERENCE

Throughout Poe's married life and after his wife's death, Maria Clemm was a strong, and not always helpful, presence. One example of the trouble she was capable of causing is her selling of a book that Poe had borrowed and asked Clemm to return to its owner, William Duane, a book collector living in Philadelphia. When Duane later wrote to ask that Poe return his borrowed volume, Poe, ignorant of Clemm's action, angrily wrote back saying that he had made arrangements for the book's return.

As a point in fact, Poe had left it to Clemm to return the book and had reminded her in his first letter to her from New York to do so. The request either fell on deaf ears or arrived too late. Clemm had sold the volume. Duane gave up trying to get the book back from Poe and began a search for a replacement copy. Several months after the exchange with Poe, he repurchased his lost book. It had been resold several times, and still bearing his autograph, had ended up where it had been published, in the hands of Poe's former employer, T. H. White.

Maria Clemm, Poe's aunt and mother-in-law, was occasionally a source of trouble for him.

Briggs followed his friend's advice, and Poe moved into New York so that he could spend time at Briggs's *Broadway Journal* offices and continue working on the *Mirror*. The *Broadway Journal*'s first issue in January 1845 carried Poe's enthusiastic review of Elizabeth Barrett's *The Drama of Exile, and Other Poems*.

NATIONWIDE FAME

Even as he began work at the *Broadway Journal*, Poe was preparing to bring "The Raven" out in a way that would gain him maximum publicity. Poe's plan was to reach the widest possible audience through several simultaneous printings and announcements of his

EDGAR AND VIRGINIA IN NEW YORK

The poet Frances Sergeant Osgood, in a memoir she wrote for Rufus W. Griswold, described Edgar Allan Poe and his wife Virginia as they appeared in their downtown home in New York City. Osgood's memoir is quoted in Arthur Hobson Quinn, Edgar Allan Poe: A Critical Biography.

"It was in his own simple yet poetical home that, to me the character of Edgar Poe appeared in its most beautiful light. Playful, affectionate, witty, alternately docile and wayward as a petted child—for his young, gentle, and idolized wife, and for all who came, he had even in the midst of his most harassing literary duties, a kind word, a pleasant smile, a graceful and courteous attention. At his desk . . . he would sit, hour after hour, patient, assiduous and uncomplaining, tracing, in an exquisitely clear chirography and with almost superhuman swiftness, the lightening thoughts—the 'rare and radiant' fancies as they flashed through his wonderful and ever wakeful brain. I recollect, one morning, towards the close of his residence in this city, when he seemed unusually gay and light-hearted. Virginia, his sweet wife, had written me a pressing invitation to come to them; and I, who could never resist her affectionate summons, and who enjoyed his society far more in his own home than elsewhere, hastened to Amity Street. I found him just completing his series of papers entitled 'The Literati of New-York.' 'See,' said he, displaying, in laughing triumph, several little rolls of narrow paper (he always wrote thus for the press), 'I am going to show you, by the difference of length in these, the different degrees of estimation in which I hold all you literary people. In each of these, one of you is rolled up and fully discussed. Come, Virginia, help me!' And one by one they unfolded them. At last they came to one which seemed interminable. Virginia laughingly ran to one corner of the room with one end, and her husband to the opposite with the other. 'And whose lengthened sweetness long drawn out is that?' said I. 'Hear her!' he cried, 'just as if her little vain heart didn't tell her it's herself!'"

poem. Poe arranged for the *American Whig Review* to publish the poem first, under a pseudonym, Quarles. Willis's *Mirror* would carry the poem on the front page—this time under Poe's signature—the next day, January 29, 1845.

The plan for publicity worked to everyone's benefit. The poem's appearance under a pseudonym had gotten people talking about "The Raven," and the *Mirror*'s publication under Poe's name gained Willis the credit for recognizing the real author's talent. The following week the poem was reprinted three times, in the *American Review,* the *New York Tribune,* and the *Broadway Journal.* The next few weeks saw the appearance of "The Raven" in the *Southern Literary Messenger,* and in England in the *London Critic.*

Still more positive publicity resulted from publication of Lowell's biographical sketch of Poe in *Graham's Magazine.* In his piece, Lowell praised the grace and symmetry of some of Poe's best early poems. In addition, the long biography noted the genius and industry of his literary analysis and called attention to his ability to make his weird fantasies seem real.

Poe was instantly famous the country over. "The Raven," says biographer Arthur Quinn, "made an impression probably not surpassed by that of any single piece of American poetry."[72] The story told in the poem, with its theme of lost love, appealed to readers' emotions. Poe's hypnotic rhythm, internal rhymes, and the haunting refrain of "Nevermore" imbued the poem with mysterious power.

The fame Poe had craved for so long had arrived. The excellence of "The Raven" caught the imagination of literary and nonliterary people alike. Collectors

The plaster head of Pallas Athena, the goddess of wisdom, which sat on a shelf in his study, was one source of inspiration for Poe as he wrote what would become his most famous poem, "The Raven."

sought Poe's manuscripts and his letters. Autograph hunters hounded him and even his aunt. As Allen notes, "Poe found himself actually occupying the breathless heights that he had dreamed himself upon, certainly since 1824."[73]

Now Poe was accepted by the literary establishment. He was called upon for a lecture to the New York Historical Society, where men and women of letters often came to exchange ideas, and almost three hundred people attended. The success of "The Raven" contributed to the success of other Poe works as well. The author was pleased when a prestigious publisher needed no urging to accept a collection of his poems. Wiley and Putnam in New York copyrighted Poe's ninety-one-page The Raven and Other Poems on September 12, 1845, and scheduled it for sale in November.

"The Raven" made Poe famous, and although it was reprinted numerous times without payments to Poe, its success with readers whetted his ambition. Moreover, it seemed as though financial reward for Poe's labor was at hand. Briggs and his publisher, John Bisco, offered him a third interest in the Broadway Journal. He accepted Briggs's offer of partnership, and on March 8, 1845, he was announced as co-editor of the weekly magazine. Poe relished the idea that he was now part owner of a journal whose pages, in some measure, were his own.

A CONTENTIOUS CRUSADE

Poe also used his new fame to escalate an old feud with fellow poet Henry Wadsworth Longfellow. Five years earlier, Poe had claimed that Longfellow had been guilty of plagiarism in some of his poetry. Now Poe launched a three-part series entitled "Continuation of the Voluminous History" in the Broadway Journal, in which he reiterated his accusations, saying that Longfellow's plagiarisms were "too palpable to be mistaken."[74]

Why Poe should have taken on such a crusade in the first place is uncertain. Biographer Jeffrey Meyers explains Poe's attacks on Longfellow as an attempt to "stir up controversy and attract readers to the Broadway Journal," as well as to justify his own "propensity to steal ideas, plots and phrases from other authors."[75] Furthermore, writes Meyers, "Poe, eternally overworked and underpaid, resented Longfellow's [well-paid professorship] at Harvard and his marriage to a wealthy woman."[76]

PERSISTENT ADVERSARIES

Yet, persistent adversaries confronted Poe. At the Broadway Journal office, Poe's periodic problem with alcohol once again worked against him. Under the influence of alcohol, Poe would turn mean. The same man who treated people with uniform kindness when he entered the office in the morning would, following an occasional whiskey after lunch, become so pugnacious that he would throw visitors out of his office with curses and insults.

Such behavior was all that Poe's old enemy Rufus Griswold needed to take up the case against him. Griswold spread many stories, often exaggerated, about the poet's bad behavior. Griswold even used the con-

POE'S LIFE AFTER "THE RAVEN"

Judge John Augustus Shea, who was present at Poe's lecture to the New York Historical Society, following the publication of "The Raven," also described his manner and appearance at the reading. These comments are quoted in Allen's Israfel.

"His reading of 'The Raven' left upon the mind a very different impression from that which it inspires in print. It was a weird, rapturous invocation as to an actual presence. Poe was among the first of the authors that took to reading and lecturing as a professional occupation. I heard him in the society library in New York in March 1845. . . . The portraits of Poe represent him with a mustache. I do not recall that he wore one when I saw him. He had a graceful walk, a beautiful olive complexion, was strikingly handsome, but had a weak chin."

tent of Poe's works against him, alleging his weird themes revealed that he was insane. Griswold's attacks became so vicious that *Godey's Lady's Book*, with no prompting, decided to publish a defense of Poe, claiming his work showed "anything but feebleness either of body or mind."[77]

Griswold's attacks also came to the attention of Poe's partners. Briggs, unwilling to believe Griswold, asked Lowell what he now thought of Poe and his work. Lowell decided to investigate, expecting to vindicate his original recommendation of Poe. With this in mind, Lowell came to call at Poe's home. That visit, unfortunately for Poe, tended only to confirm the negative stories. Lowell found Poe drunk; he left, disillusioned and unable to relieve Briggs's doubts.

Poe also did himself no favors by attacking the very people who might otherwise have defended him from Griswold.

In Philadelphia, *Godey's Lady's Book* had begun publishing his series, *The Literati of New York City: Some Honest Opinions at Random Respecting Their Authorial Merits, with Occasional Words of Personality.* In these brief descriptive sketches of fellow New York writers, Poe was often sharp in his assessment of his colleagues, even going so far as to claim that his own partner, Briggs, was uneducated.

FULL RESPONSIBILITY

Poe's partnership with Briggs was about to end for other reasons, however. Throughout its four months of publication the *Broadway Journal* had not brought in enough money to allow Briggs to pay his employees and printers, much less generate the profit he had agreed to share with his partners Bisco and Poe. After some negotiation, Bisco agreed to buy Briggs's share from him. As a result, the *Broadway Journal* came out in July 1845 with Poe's name listed as its only editor.

Still, the *Broadway Journal* made no money. With no profit to share in, Poe was nearly starving. After three months, Bisco gave up as well. He sold the bankrupt business to Poe for fifty dollars, which Poe borrowed from his colleague, editor Horace Greeley, in return for a promissory note.

END OF THE *BROADWAY JOURNAL*

As the *Broadway Journal*'s proprietor, Poe made full use of the editorial freedom that ownership gave him. Under pressure to keep expenses to a minimum, he effectively became the journal's only contributor. Getting the paper ready to print greatly limited the time he had for writing, but he still managed to compose some new reviews. Mostly, however, he meticulously revised and reprinted a large number of his earlier works.

The *Broadway Journal*'s weekly payroll, printing, and distribution were also Poe's responsibility, but he had no money. In a vain attempt to save the magazine from bankruptcy, he returned to the kind of begging correspondence he had once carried on with John Allan. Approaching friends and acquaintances for ten dollars here, twenty-five dollars there, one hundred dollars somewhere else, he tried to stave off the journal's inevitable demise.

Finally, unable to pay the printers and typesetters, Poe issued the final issue of the *Broadway Journal* on January 3, 1846, hardly

six months after Bisco's offer of partnership. In all, the time Poe had spent on the journal had resulted in almost no real income. One scholar, John Ward Ostrom, analyzes Poe's finances for the year this way:

> Throughout 1845 besides general activities for the *Journal*, Poe earned $130 from contributions to it; he also wrote for other magazines: *Godey's* bought one tale and four articles; the *Democratic Review* one tale; Colton's *American Review*, two tales, two articles, and one poem; *Graham's* a short story—in all $197. For the year he apparently made $549. But because he had borrowed $135 from Wiley and Putnam against royalties on his *Tales* in 1845, he actually owed his publisher $15. This kind of indebtedness was typical, as were his attempts to borrow even more on the same royalties and on a projected title (*Literary America*) that was never completed. It seems only proper to add here that some people like Fitz-Green Halleck, a New York writer who loaned Poe money, really never expected to be repaid.[78]

Ever able to put his failures in the best possible light, Poe wrote this farewell: "Unexpected engagements demanding my whole attention, and the objects being fulfilled, so far as regards myself personally, for which the *Broadway Journal* was established, I now, as its editor, bid farewell—as cordially to foes as to friends."[79] Another aspect of Poe's life was also coming to an end, and even more than the *Broadway Journal*'s closing, this would leave Poe devastated.

Chapter

7 Personal Cost

Poe's struggles over keeping the *Broadway Journal* alive paralleled Virginia's losing battle with tuberculosis. At home downtown in their tiny apartment, suffering from the heat in the summer and cold in the winter, she bore her privations bravely. Despite his best efforts, Poe was only able to bring home a little money for her and her mother.

Closing the *Broadway Journal,* however, left Poe with no reason to live in downtown New York City. The family moved back to the house they had rented from the Brennans, then, for a short time to a house located on 47th Street. Eventually, in late April 1846, for one hundred dollars a year, Poe rented a cottage in the village of Fordham, located about thirteen miles north of the city.

The move improved the family's physical environment for the summer months, but socially Poe and those around him were being ostracized. His gossipy sketches of his colleagues had alienated people who might otherwise have been friendly or helpful. Increasingly, those he had profiled replied in print with attacks of their own. In a letter to his friend, Dr. Thomas H. Chivers, Poe, on July 22, 1846, alluded to the spreading ill will that was adding to his misery:

We are in a snug little cottage, keeping house, and would be very comfortable, but that I have been for a long time dreadfully ill. I am getting better, however, though slowly, and shall get *well.* In the meantime the flocks of little birds of prey that always take the opportunity of illness to peck at a sick foul of large dimensions, have been endeavoring with all their power to effect my ruin. My dreadful poverty, also, has given them every advantage. In fact, my dear friend, I have been driven to the very gates of death and a despair more dreadful than death, and I had not even *one* friend, out of my family, with whom to advise. What would I not have given for the kind pressure of your hand! It is only a few days since that I requested my mother in law, Mrs. Clemm, to write to you—but she put it off from day to day.[80]

Poe noted, however, that for his part, he was making an effort to reform his personal behavior, which he knew was contributing to his problems:

There is one thing you will be glad to learn:—It has been a long while since

In 1846, Poe rented this home in Fordham, New York, for one hundred dollars a year.

any artificial stimulus has passed my lips. When I see you—should that day ever come—this is a topic on which I desire to have a long talk with you. I am done forever with drink—depend upon that—but there is much more in this matter than meets the eye.[81]

In spite of his efforts to modify his behavior, Poe was the eventual victim of his own acid wit. One of Poe's targets, a poet named Thomas Dunn English, wrote a devastating satire of Poe. English's thinly disguised character of Hammerhead was widely seen by readers as lampooning Poe's drinking habits:

> [Hammerhead's] bloated face—blood-shotten eyes—trembling fingers and attenuated frame, showed how rapidly he was sinking into a drunkard's grave; and the drivelling smile, and meaningless nonsense he constantly uttered, showed the approaching wreck of his fine abilities. Delirium tremens . . . was rapidly followed by confirmed insanity, or rather monomania. He deemed himself the object of persecution on the part

of the combined literati of the country, and commenced writing criticism upon their character as writers, and their peculiarities as men. In this he gave the first inkling of his insanity, by discovering that there were over eighty eminent writers in the city of New York.[82]

Poe replied to English's attack by suing him for libel. The fact was that people believed that the description in English's satire was accurate. Poe won the suit and was awarded $225 in damages.

Poe's sketches eventually harmed their author financially. A few of his New York readers, such as the editor Horace Greeley, continued to be amused by Poe's pieces but eventually the controversial nature of the sketches caused the editor to stop publishing them.

POE'S HOME IN FORDHAM

During the summer of 1846 a family friend, Mrs. Mary Gove Nichols, visited the Poes at their home in Fordham. Her recollection of the appearance of the home was first quoted in a memoir by Poe's admirer Susan Archer Weiss and appears in Arthur Hobson Quinn's Edgar Allan Poe: A Critical Biography.

"We made one excursion to Fordham to see Poe. We found him, and his wife, and his wife's mother—who was his aunt—living in a little cottage at the top of a hill. There was an acre or two of greensward, fenced in about the house, as smooth as velvet and as clean as the best kept carpet. There were some grand old cherry trees in the yard, that threw a massive shade around them. The house had three rooms—a kitchen, a sitting-room, and a bed-chamber over the sitting-room. There was a piazza in front of the house that was a lovely place to sit in in summer, with the shade of cherry-trees before it, there was no cultivation, no flowers—nothing but the smooth greensward and the majestic trees. . . .

The cottage had an air of taste and gentility that must have been lent to it by the presence of its inmates. So neat, so poor, so unfurnished, and yet so charming a dwelling I never saw. The floor of the kitchen was white as wheaten flour. A table, a chair, and a little stove that it contained, seemed to furnish it perfectly. The sitting-room floor was laid with check matting; four chairs, a light stand, and a hanging bookshelf completed its furniture. There were pretty presentation copies of books on the little shelves, and the Brownings had posts of honour on the stand. With quiet exultation Poe drew from his side pocket a letter that he had recently received from Elizabeth Barrett Browning. He read it to us. It was very flattering. She told Poe that his 'poem of the Raven had awakened a fit of horror in England.'"

For his part, Poe rationalized a situation that he had brought on himself, saying he had decided to renew his efforts to start a magazine of his own. Still calling his publication the *Stylus*, he planned to reach beyond the narrow literary interests of any one city, be it New York, Boston, Philadelphia, Baltimore, or Richmond. He wrote in his 1846 prospectus that the magazine would provide an impartial forum for literary people to present their views to a national readership.

A NOTICE IN THE PAPERS

Beyond the controversy over his biographical sketches, Poe had a far more serious worry: Virginia's death was obviously near, and there was nothing he could do to prevent it. Moreover, he was unable to provide even the barest necessities for his family.

The desperation of the Poes' situation was made public in the December 15, 1846, edition of the *New York Morning Express*. A volunteer nurse from Greenwich Village, Mrs. Marie Louise Shew, and some other ladies who had been visiting Virginia at the cottage in Fordham became so disturbed over the lack of food and heat in the house that they put a plea for help in the newspaper. The notice read:

> We regret to learn that [Poe] and his wife are both dangerously ill with the consumption, and . . . [w]e are sorry to mention the fact that they are so far reduced as to be barely able to obtain the necessaries of life. That is indeed a hard lot, and we do hope that the friends and admirers of Mr. Poe will

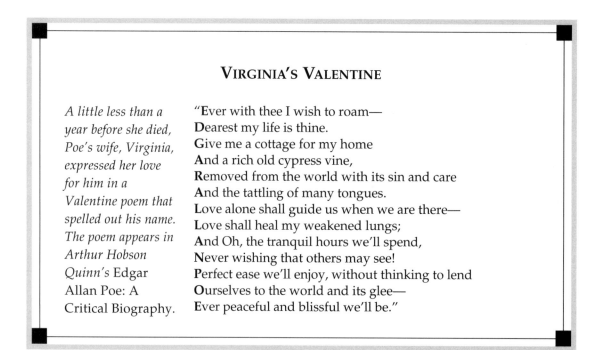

VIRGINIA'S VALENTINE

A little less than a year before she died, Poe's wife, Virginia, expressed her love for him in a Valentine poem that spelled out his name. The poem appears in Arthur Hobson Quinn's Edgar Allan Poe: A Critical Biography.

"Ever with thee I wish to roam—
Dearest my life is thine.
Give me a cottage for my home
And a rich old cypress vine,
Removed from the world with its sin and care
And the tattling of many tongues.
Love alone shall guide us when we are there—
Love shall heal my weakened lungs;
And Oh, the tranquil hours we'll spend,
Never wishing that others may see!
Perfect ease we'll enjoy, without thinking to lend
Ourselves to the world and its glee—
Ever peaceful and blissful we'll be."

come promptly to his assistance in his bitterest hour of need.[83]

Poe denied the report of his own illness, but he decided not to refuse help if it were offered. In particular he accepted the medical assistance of Mrs. Shew, who was making it her business to minister regularly to Virginia. She also served as something of a confidante to Poe himself, in hopes of helping him overcome his grief over the death that was soon to come.

In a letter Poe expressed his gratitude to Shew for her help:

> My poor Virginia still lives, although failing fast and now suffering much pain. May God grant her life until she sees you and thanks you once again! Her bosom is full to overflowing—like my own—with a boundless—inexpressible gratitude to you. Lest she may never see you more—she bids me say that she sends you her sweetest kiss of love and will die blessing you.[84]

UNUTTERABLE LOSS

Virginia died on January 30, 1847, attended by kind and charitable women and comforted by the addition of a few warm coverings and some nourishing food during her last days. The funeral on February 2 was attended by several women, including Mrs. Shew and the Poes' cousin Mrs. Elizabeth Herring Smith, and the editor Nathaniel Parker Willis. For Poe, the loss of his wife was devastating, and he himself finally fell ill.

One of Poe's supporters, Horace Greeley, accused him of being untrustworthy and of acting in bad faith because of Poe's failure to repay a debt.

Once again Mrs. Shew used her medical knowledge and analyzed Poe's condition. Her observations, relayed to her supervisor, Dr. Valentine Mott, mentioned that he had what she called brain fever "brought on by extreme suffering of mind and body—actual want and hunger, and cold . . . [and] that even sedatives had to be administered with extreme caution."[85]

In addition to being dangerously ill, Poe was under public attack, this time as being untrustworthy when it came to repaying debts. Horace Greeley, who had been one of Poe's supporters when his sketches of New York writers were generating such controversy, now accused Poe

SETTING UP A LECTURE

A recurrent theme in Poe's life was his need to rely on friends and acquaintances for money or favors. On January 18, 1848, Poe wrote to H. D. Chapin at the New York Society to arrange for a room for his lecture on "The Universe," while asking that the society make an exception to its policy of requiring advance payment. This excerpt is quoted in The Poe Log, *edited by Dwight Thomas and David K. Jackson.*

"Mrs. Shew intimated to me, not long ago, that you would, perhaps, lend me your aid in my endeavour to re-establish myself in the literary world. . . . When I last spoke with you, I mentioned my design of going to see Mr. [John] Neal at Portland, and there, with his influence, deliver a Lecture—the proceeds of which might enable me to take the first steps towards my proposed Magazine—that is to say, put, perhaps, $100 in my pocket; which would give me the necessary outfit and start me on my tour. But, since our conversation, I have been thinking that a better course would be to make interest among my friends here—in N.Y. City—and deliver a Lecture, in the first instance, at the Society Library. With this object in view, may I beg of you so far to assist me as to procure for me the use of the Lecture Room? The difficulty with me is that payment for the room is demanded *in advance* and I have no money. I believe the price is $15."

of bad faith. Poe, Greeley charged, owed him fifty dollars, borrowed to buy the *Broadway Journal*. Greeley also accused Poe of having borrowed the money with no intention of ever paying it back.

To Greeley, Poe responded,

> I owe you money—I have been ill, unfortunate, no doubt weak, and as yet unable to refund the money— but on this ground *you*, Mr. Greeley, would never have accused me of being habitually "unscrupulous in the fulfillment of my pecuniary engagements." The charge is *horribly false*— I have a hundred times left myself destitute of bread for myself and family that I might discharge debts.[86]

Poe began to recover his health and returned to writing poetry. To honor Marie Louise Shew, he composed "The Beloved Physician." Although he had intended it for publication, the poem did not appear because Shew purchased the manuscript from him. For the eighth edition of *The Poets and Poetry of America* he revised "The Landscape Garden" and offered its editor—his old nemesis Rufus Griswold—the honor of reprinting his most famous poems, "The Raven," "The Conqueror Worm," "The Coliseum," "The Haunted Palace," and "The Sleeper."

The Plot of God

Eventually, Poe recovered from his illness. By the beginning of 1848, he was back to work, full of enthusiasm. He now had a name for a long prose poem he had been composing, *Eureka* (Greek for "I have found it!"). Through this poem, Poe expounded his theory that everything created in the world affects everything else in creation. To look at the divine construction of the universe, he said, is to see that "The plots of God are perfect. The Universe is a plot of God."[87]

As he developed this lengthy work, Poe relied on his aunt's moral support. Mrs. Clemm later reported that they "used to walk up and down the garden, his arm around me, mine around him, until I was so tired I could not walk."[88] Poe quickly found a publisher for this new work. By May 19, he was proofreading a copy of *Eureka: A Prose Poem* for the publisher George P. Putnam. The small volume, priced at seventy-five cents and printed in an edition of 750 copies, was issued in the middle of July 1848.

Eureka was reviewed immediately by James Brooks of the *Morning Express,* who declared it an extraordinary work. Brooks said its novelty and importance would probably "create a most profound sensation among the literary and scientific classes all over the Union" for its "logical acumen which has certainly not been equalled since the days of Sir Isaac Newton."[89] At least twenty other reviews followed, predicting varying degrees of success for *Eureka.*

As with much of Poe's work, this poem generated its share of controversy. Many saw *Eureka* as a treatise promoting a new theory of the universe rather than as a poem. To members of the clergy and others concerned about morality, the view of creation expressed in the work seemed shocking. Even so, five hundred copies sold during the year.

A Mixed Blessing

After the publication of *Eureka,* Poe began a series of lectures to promote it. Following one of these lectures, delivered in June 1848, in Lowell, Massachusetts, north of Boston, Poe attended a reception at which he met Annie Richmond, the wife of Charles Richmond, a paper manufacturer.

Poe was quite enamored of Annie, and the attraction was mutual. But the relationship never went beyond friendship, since Annie was happily married. Still, Annie became one of Poe's staunchest supporters. Years later, she wrote to Poe's biographer John Ingram, "He seemed so *unlike* any other person I had ever known, that I could not think of him in the same way—he was incomparable—not to be measured by any ordinary standard."[90]

Other relationships showed promise of going beyond mere friendship. Shortly after meeting Annie Richmond, Poe took the advice of his nurse Marie Louise Shew to seek a marriage that would supply him with the calm and steady affection a wife could provide. Toward this end, he courted the poet Sarah Helen Whitman, a widow who lived with her mother in Providence, Rhode Island. Whitman agreed to meet him formally in her mother's parlor, on September 21,

Love Letter to Sarah Helen Whitman

Poe's letters to the woman he was courting, Sarah Helen Whitman, show the passion and abandon of his emotions for her. Excerpted here from The Letters of Edgar Allan Poe, *edited by John Ward Ostrom, is his first letter to Whitman, written on October 1, 1848.*

"Do you not feel in your inmost heart of hearts that the 'soul-love' of which the world speaks so often and so idly is, in this instance at least, but the veriest, the most absolute of realities? Do you not—I ask it of your reason, darling, not less than of your heart—do you not perceive that it is my diviner nature—my spiritual being—which burns and pants to commingle with your own? Has the soul age, Helen? Can Immortality regard Time? Can that which began never and shall never end, consider a few wretched years of its incarnate life? . . . Has not my heart ceased to throb beneath the magic of your smile? Have I not held your hand in mine and looked steadily into your soul through the crystal Heaven of your eyes? Have I not done all these things?—or do I dream?—or am I mad? Were you indeed all that your fancy, enfeebled and perverted by illness, tempts you to suppose that you are, still, life of my life! I would but love you—but worship you the more."

Poe's relationship with poet Sarah Helen Whitman ended when he was observed under the influence of alcohol.

1848. The couple met as planned, and ten days later, in the first of several love letters he wrote, Poe told Whitman that he saw in her the embodiment of his fantasies.

Poe visited Whitman and her mother on several occasions in their home. He promised Whitman that he would give up alcohol and gave her a daguerreotype of himself, taken at her request. But the relationship ended before the couple could marry, although newspapers reported that they planned to do so. Whitman's mother, convinced that Poe was mostly after her money, opposed the marriage. Moreover, Poe soon broke his promise of staying away from alcohol. January of 1848 found both Poe and Whitman drawing back from the relationship.

Chapter

8 A Mysterious Death

By early 1849, Poe had put his brief relationship with Sarah Helen Whitman behind him. Now he once again devoted his energy to work, writing two poems: "Annabel Lee," which scholars see as honoring the memory of Virginia, and "Eldorado," which was about the fever generated by the discovery of gold in California that same year.

INSPIRED BY THE GOLD RUSH

Like the protagonist in "Eldorado," Poe pursued his goals with new vigor and declared, "I shall be a *littérateur,* (lover of literature) at least, all my life; nor would I abandon the hopes which still lead me on for all the gold in California."[91]

The gold rush also inspired Poe's tale "Von Kempelen and His Discovery," a whimsical hoax relating how the chemical process for changing lead into gold had been lost. The writing of this tale was, as Poe characterized it, "a kind of 'exercise,' or experiment, in the plausible or verisimilar style. Of course, there is *not one* word of truth in it from beginning to end."[92]

The monetary returns for his two gold-rush pieces were modest at best, but they helped Poe get on his feet. The magazine

Flag of Our Union purchased "Von Kempelen" at a rate of five dollars per page, then paid the same for three more new stories, published between March and June of 1849. They were "Hop-Frog," a tale of morbid revenge; "Landor's Cottage," a quiet, reflective essay describing Annie Richmond, his Fordham home and the surrounding countryside; and "X-ing a Paragrab," a hilarious spoof on typesetters. The same magazine also paid Poe five dollars each for "Eldorado," and a revision of another poem, "A Valentine."

AN OFFER OF SUPPORT FOR THE *STYLUS*

In addition to the positive response to his poetry and fiction from the *Flag of Our Union,* Poe received good news from a journalist, Edward Howard Norton Patterson, editor of the *Oquawka Spectator,* published near Peoria, Illinois. Patterson offered substantial monetary support for the publication of the *Stylus.*

Poe's response to this unexpected offer was cautious. This was a time when other magazines, like the *Democratic Review,* the *Metropolitan,* and the *Columbian* were in such difficult financial straits that they could not pay for contributions or were going out of business because of lack of funds. Even *Flag of Our Union* suddenly suspended publication—a blow to Poe's income.

Energized, nevertheless, by Patterson's offer, Poe wrote on May 23 to express his interest and his reservations: he felt that the New York office from which the *Stylus* was to be operated was too far away from Oquawka to make the situation workable. Still, Poe proposed that publication begin in 1850, which left seven months for preparation. For his part, Poe said, he was on his way to Richmond in early June to lecture and solicit subscriptions among his friends and acquaintances there.

Delayed by Illness

On his way to Richmond, however, Poe spent more than three weeks seriously ill in Philadelphia. The experience threw him once again into despair. Finally able to resume his journey on July 7, 1849, despite still feeling ill, he wrote to Maria Clemm saying, "I have had the cholera or spasms quite as bad," he wrote, "and can now hardly hold the pen."[93] Poe also complained of hallucinations, although he claimed that he was not drinking.

When Poe finally arrived in Richmond, a letter from Patterson awaited him with a fifty-dollar advance on the *Stylus*. Feeling somewhat recovered, Poe wrote to thank Patterson and explain that his illness had kept him from writing earlier. To Clemm he confessed that his problem had been

partly due to drinking but that the extremity of his illness was a warning that would keep him from ever drinking again.

The gold rush that drew huge numbers of men like these to California inspired Poe to write "Eldorado" and "Von Kempelen and His Discovery."

"Ride, Boldly Ride"

Edgar Allan Poe was inspired to write this enigmatic poem when he heard of the 1849 gold strike in California. It is included in Poe's Selected Tales and Poems, *edited by Hervey Allen.*

Eldorado

Gaily bedight,
A gallant knight,
In sunshine and in shadow,
Had journeyed long,
Singing a song,
In search of Eldorado.

But he grew old—
This knight so bold—
And o'er his heart a shadow
Fell as he found
No spot of ground
That looked like Eldorado.

And as his strength
Failed him at length,
He met a pilgrim shadow—
"Shadow," said he,
"Where can it be—
This land of Eldorado?"

Over the Mountains
Of the Moon,
Down the Valley of the Shadow,
"Ride, boldly ride,"
The shade replied,
"If you search for Eldorado."

BACK IN RICHMOND

Poe's stated purpose in coming to Richmond, to generate publicity for the *Stylus,* was slowly accomplished. He was able to arrange to give a lecture. He made several visits to the *Southern Literary Messenger* and to the *Richmond Examiner,* to request notices and news coverage of his effort. In his spare time, he worked on revising *Eureka* and on a satirical article, "The Reviewer Reviewed."

Biographer Thomas Ollive Mabbott summarizes this period for Poe as

the Indian summer of his life. He was now received into society, and we have pleasant reminiscences of his attendance at the Mackenzies', where he saw his sister Rosalie and mingled with young people and even children, who usually liked him. Other friends were his childhood "little sweetheart" Catherine Poitiaux, Robert Stanard, Robert Sully the painter, Dr. Robert Henry Cabell and his wife Julia Mayo Cabell (a cousin of the second Mrs. John Allan), Dr. John F. Carter and Thomas Alfriend and his son Edward. Poe called almost daily on Susan Archer Talley, a poetess of eighteen, whom he trusted and regarded with such affection that he instructed his friends to watch him to make sure she never saw him when he was not himself.[94]

Poe delivered his talk, "The Poetic Principle," on August 7, 1849, and it was received with such enthusiasm that some in his audience encouraged him to charge

While in Richmond in 1849 to generate publicity for the Stylus, *Poe gave several lectures which were met with great enthusiasm.*

fifty cents a ticket for his lectures instead of the customary twenty-five cents. He scheduled a repeat of the lecture in Norfolk, Virginia, on September 14, and again in Richmond on September 24.

FIRST LOVE REVISITED

Along with promoting the *Stylus*, Poe also made a point of visiting Elmira Royster Shelton, his childhood sweetheart, now widowed. Two barriers, however, stood in the way of his renewing their relationship: Elmira was opposed to the drinking of alcohol, and her family members—brothers George, James, and Alexander Royster, and her two children—were strongly opposed to her having anything to do with Poe.

Soon after his successful lecture, Poe managed to overcome the first barrier to Elmira's friendship. On August 27, he took the temperance pledge in the Shockoe Hill Division No. 54 of the Sons of Temperance. His initiation and pledge not to touch liquor were duly reported in the organization's newsletter on August 31 and repeated as news in Richmond's newspaper, the *Daily Republican,* on September 1.

Right after Poe took the pledge he wrote to Clemm that he and his sister Rosalie were planning to spend the evening at Elmira's and that she had said she would like to visit Fordham to meet Clemm. Plans for marriage to Elmira had even developed to the point of Poe's announcing that he had a wedding ring and was hoping he'd be able to afford a dress coat.

Still, the barrier of the Royster family's opposition remained. The family had reservations about Poe's character and also believed that he was mostly after the money Elmira's late husband had left her. Shelton had provided protection against such gold digging in his will, which read in part, "If my wife shall marry again then immediately upon the happening of that event I do hereby . . . request that the Court will . . . require her to deliver up my estate from her possession and management."[95] Still, Elmira's family persisted in their opposition.

PLANS GO AHEAD

Elmira, however, seemed not to care about either the loss of her inheritance or what her brothers or her children thought of Poe. She wrote to Clemm telling her how much she looked forward to meeting her. In a letter to Clemm, on September 18, Poe indicated that plans for the wedding were going forward and that the next time he came to New York he would again be a married man:

> Elmira has just got home from the country. I spent last evening with her. I think she loves me more devotedly than any one I ever knew & I cannot help loving her in return. Nothing is yet definitely settled . . . and it will not do to hurry matters. I lectured at Norfolk on Monday & cleared enough to settle my bill here at the Madison House with $2 over. . . .
>
> If possible I will get married before I start [to New York] . . . I showed your letter to Elmira and she says "it is

POE'S SOBRIETY IN RICHMOND

Poe retained his ability to charm others right up to the end of his life. On Sunday, September 9, 1849, he attended a party near Richmond, and one of the women there, Susan V. Ingram, later recalled him as a courteous and charming gentleman. Ingram's account is quoted in the "Memoir" of J. H. Whitty, accompanying The Complete Poems of Edgar Allan Poe.

"When we . . . requested . . . that he recite for us he agreed readily. He recited 'The Raven,' 'Annabel Lee' and last of all 'Ulalume,' with the last stanza of which he remarked that he feared it might not be intelligible to us, as it was scarcely clear to himself, and for that reason it had not been published. The next day he sent a copy of the poem with a letter.

We went from Old Point Comfort to our home near Norfolk, and he called on us there, and again I had the pleasure of talking with him. Although I was only a slip of a girl and he what then seemed to me quite an old man, and a great literary one at that, we got on together beautifully. He was one of the most courteous gentlemen I have ever seen, and that gave a great charm to his manner. None of his pictures that I have ever seen look like the picture of Poe that I keep in my memory. Of course they look like him, so that any one seeing them could have recognized him from them, but there was something in his face that is in none of them. Perhaps it was in the eyes, perhaps in the mouth. I do not know, but any one who ever met him would understand what I mean.

There were no indications of dissipation apparent when we saw Poe in Virginia at that time. I think he had not been drinking for a long time. If I had not heard or read what had been said about his intemperance I should never have had any idea of it from what I saw in Poe. To me he seemed a good man, as well as a charming one, very sensitive and high minded."

such a darling precious letter that she loves you for it already."[96]

For reasons that are unclear, and in spite of the hopeful tone of his letter, while he was in Richmond Poe had been making a kind of will. He had engaged an editor to see to the publication of his works if he should die suddenly. Surprisingly, Poe had offered that responsibility to his old enemy, Rufus Griswold. The Richmond poet Susan Archer Talley Weiss later reported that Griswold "accepted the proposal, expressing himself as much flattered thereby, and writing in terms of friendly warmth and interest."[97]

A Short Trip to New York

Ultimately, Poe decided to make the trip to New York before the wedding. The husband of a Philadelphia poet, Mrs. Marguerite Loud, had offered to pay Poe one hundred dollars to edit one of his wife's manuscripts for publication. The cash would be a welcome help for bringing Clemm to Richmond and helping with the needs of Poe and his new wife.

With Griswold in place as his literary executor and his plans to marry Elmira moving forward, the calm and steadiness Poe needed seemed to be at hand. He prepared to leave for New York on September 25, the day after he was scheduled to deliver his third lecture. He would stop in Philadelphia to edit Mrs. Loud's book and receive his one hundred dollars.

Poe spent the 25th in Richmond. He visited friends and stopped at the offices of the *Southern Literary Messenger* to give the editor, John R. Thompson, a manuscript of "Annabel Lee" in return for a loan of five dollars. Poe also agreed to deliver a letter from Thompson to Griswold in Philadelphia. Thompson later reported that Poe left the *Messenger* offices in good spirits.

Next, Poe went to Elmira's to say good-bye. Her impression of her fiance's condition was quite different from Thompson's: "He complained of being quite sick; I felt his pulse, and found he had considerable fever, and did not think it probable that he would be able to start the next morning, as he anticipated."[98] Contrary to Elmira's expectations, Poe left as scheduled. About 9:30 in the evening, Poe visited the office of his friend Dr. John Carter, where he read the newspapers. He had supper at Sadler's Restaurant and then went to the boat to await its departure. The boat trip would take twenty-four hours, and Poe was planning to arrive in Baltimore early on September 27, 1849.

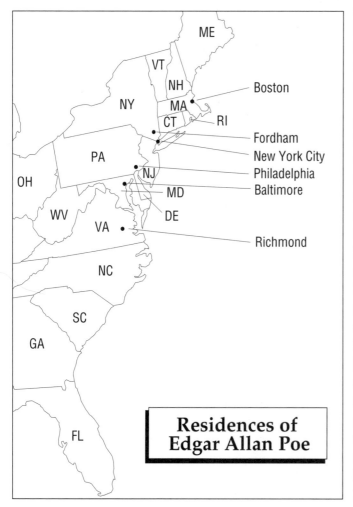

ME
VT
NH
NY
MA — Boston
CT
RI
Fordham
New York City
PA
NJ
Philadelphia
Baltimore
OH
MD
WV
DE
VA
Richmond
NC
SC
GA
FL

Residences of Edgar Allan Poe

According to John Sartain, Poe did arrive in Philadelphia. Looking haggard, Poe had come to Sartain's office seeking protection and shelter.

A MYSTERIOUS TURNAROUND

Poe's boat arrived in Baltimore in the morning. He had a three-hour wait before his scheduled 9:00 A.M. train to Philadelphia. At this point, Poe's movements become a mystery. A train conductor reported seeing him board the train for Philadelphia. But that same conductor was surprised to see Poe soon returning on the same car going back to Baltimore, when instead he should have taken the boat across the Susquehanna River for the connecting train on to Philadelphia.

One thing that is known for certain is that Poe failed to keep his appointment in Philadelphia at the home of Mrs. Loud. A Philadelphia friend, the engraver John Sartain, indicates, however, that Poe eventually did arrive in Philadelphia. Sartain was surprised by a furtive visit from the poet, which he recounted in 1879 in *Lippincott's Magazine:*

> The last time I saw Mr. Poe was in 1849, and then under such peculiar and fearful conditions that it can never fade from my memory. Early

one Monday afternoon he suddenly made his appearance in my engraving-room, looking pale and haggard and with a wild expression in his eyes. I did not let him see that I had noticed it, and shaking his hand warmly, invited him to be seated, when he began, "Mr. Sartain, I have come to you for protection and refuge. It will be difficult for you to believe what I have to tell—that such things could be in this nineteenth century. It is necessary that I remain concealed for a time. Can I stay here with you?"

"Certainly," said I, "as long as you like: you will be perfectly safe here." He thanked me and then went into an explanation of what was the matter.

He said that he was on his way to New York, when he overheard some men who sat a few seats back of him plotting how they would kill him and throw him from the platform of the car. He said they spoke so low it would have been impossible for him to hear and understand the meaning of their words, had it not been that his sense of hearing was so acute. They did not guess that he had heard them, as he sat so quiet and suppressed all indication of having heard the plot.[99]

Sartain went on to retell Poe's story of how he had managed to get off the train a short distance out of Philadelphia without being seen by the plotters and returned to town. Asked why anybody would want to kill him, Poe told Sartain the reason was trouble over a woman.

Then Poe suggested he might escape the men unrecognized if he shaved off his mustache, which Sartain did for him using a pair of scissors.

A second report also places Poe in Philadelphia. An aunt of Thomas H. Lane, the former bookkeeper of the *Broadway Journal*, reported taking care of Poe overnight on an unspecified date and that he had left, taking the train back to Baltimore.

THE MYSTERY DEEPENS

No record exists of Poe's whereabouts either the weekend after his boat arrived in Baltimore nor the day following his Monday visit to Sartain. The next recorded event in Poe's travels was his awakening on Wednesday morning, October 3, very sick, at Ryan's tavern in Baltimore. A reporter and printer friend, Joseph Walker, who had been alerted by an anonymous message, came over to talk with him. Poe asked him to get help from his friend, Joseph Evans Snodgrass, who lived only two blocks away.

Not finding Snodgrass at home, Walker left a note, saying that his friend was "rather the worse for wear, at Ryan's 4th ward polls, . . . appears in great distress, & says he is acquainted with you, and I assure you, he is in need of immediate assistance."[100] Walker also contacted Poe's cousin, Neilson Poe.

Neilson Poe, Snodgrass, and the Reverend William T. D. Clemm, a cousin of Virginia's, all arrived at Ryan's tavern at about the same time just before 5:00 P.M. William Clemm later recalled:

[I] instantly recognized the face of one whom I had often seen and knew well, although it wore an aspect of vacant stupidity which made me shudder . . . perhaps I would not have so readily recognized him had I not been notified of his apparel. His hat—or rather the hat of somebody else, for he had evidently been robbed of his clothing, or cheated in an exchange—was a cheap palm leaf one, without a band, and soiled, his coat, of commonest alpaca, and evident "second hand"; and his pants of gray-mixed cassimere, dingy and badly fitting. He wore neither vest nor neckcloth, if I remember aright, while his shirt was sadly crumpled and soiled.[101]

Poe clearly needed to be hospitalized. By now unconscious, he was brought to Washington College Hospital and examined by Dr. John J. Moran, the attending physician. Poe did not regain consciousness until three o'clock Thursday morning, when he went into tremors and delirium. Pale and perspiring, he talked without making sense for more than twenty-four hours.

As soon as he felt Poe could respond, Moran questioned him, but found him incoherent about what had become of his trunk or his clothing. Moran reassured him he would be well taken care of and would recover, but at this suggestion, says Moran,

[Poe] broke out with much energy and said the best thing his best friend

---

CLEMM BEGS FROM GRISWOLD

Maria Clemm displayed the same willingness as her nephew to borrow money to meet her needs. In this letter, quoted in Joseph Wood Krutch, Edgar Allan Poe: A Study in Genius, *Clemm complains to Rufus Griswold of her circumstances and asks Poe's enemy for a loan.*

"I feel that you will pardon the liberty I take in addressing you, but the extreme urgency of my situation compels me to do so. Mr. Poe has been absent from home for some weeks; he is now in Richmond and has been very ill, and unable to send me any money since he left, and is much distressed for fear of my suffering. Indeed I *have suffered.* I have been very sick, and entirely unable to make the least exertion. I have been without the necessaries of life for many days, and would not apply to anyone, in hopes that I would soon receive some aid from my poor Eddy. He writes me that he is getting better, and hopes he will soon be able to attend to business. I confide in you, dear sir, and beg you to lend me a small sum until I can receive some from him. I have not the means to go to the city, but a note addressed to Mrs. Maria Clemm, care of E. A. Poe, New York will reach me. A gentleman in the neighborhood asks every day for me at the post office."

Edgar Allan Poe's burial place in the Westminster Church cemetery in Baltimore was enhanced by the addition of this memorial stone in 1876.

could do would be to blow his brains out with a pistol—that when he beheld his degradation he was ready to sink in the earth, etc. Shortly after giving expression to these words Mr. Poe seemed to [doze] & I left him for a short time.

When I returned I found him [in] a violent delirium, resisting the efforts of two nurses to keep him in bed.[102]

An Unexpected Death

The rest of Thursday night, all day Friday, and until Saturday evening, Poe continued in violent delirium, recounts Moran. Exhausted but still delirious, he called incessantly for someone named Reynolds.

At three o'clock on Sunday morning, October 7, continues Moran, "a very decided change began to affect him. Having become enfeebled from exertion he became quiet and seemed to rest for a short time, then gently moving his head he said *'Lord help my poor soul'* and expired!"[103]

Poe's cousin, Neilson Poe, and Henry Herring, another cousin, were notified on Sunday morning. "I was never so much shocked, in my life" wrote Neilson Poe, "as when, on Sunday morning, notice was sent to me that he was dead."[104] Neilson Poe hired a hearse, and Herring furnished a coffin. Moran asked the Reverend Clemm of Caroline Street Methodist Episcopal Church to conduct the funeral.

The funeral procession left Washington College Hospital at 4:00 P.M. on Monday, October 8. An onlooker, Charles William Hubner, then fourteen years old, asked who was being buried. He was told, "My son, that is the body of a great poet, Edgar Allan Poe, you will learn all about him some day."[105]

Clemm's church service was attended by Poe's cousins Neilson Poe and Henry Herring; his friend Joseph Evans Snodgrass; and Z. Collins Lee, a University of Virginia classmate who was living in Baltimore at the time.

Poe was buried in the cemetery of Westminster Church in Baltimore, in the same lot with his grandfather, General David Poe. Attending the graveside service were Poe's first cousin Elizabeth Rebecca Herring with her husband, Edmund Morron Smith; the church sexton George W. Spence; the undertaker Charles Suter; and Poe's Richmond schoolmaster, Joseph H. Clarke. An

---

ANNIE RICHMOND COMFORTS MARIA CLEMM AFTER POE'S DEATH

On October 10, 1849, Mrs. Annie Richmond wrote to Mrs. Clemm at Fordham, to comfort her in the news of Edgar's death and offer her a home. Richmond's suggestion that Clemm bring along Poe's papers and books suggests that she foresaw a time when these items would become valuable. The letter appears in Dwight Thomas and David K. Jackson, The Poe Log.

"Oh my mother, my darling darling mother oh what shall I say to you—how *can* I comfort you. . . . if I could only have laid down *my* life for his, that he might have been spared to you—but mother it is the will of God, and we must submit, and Heaven grant us strength, to bear it. . . . your letter [of yesterday] has this moment reached me, but I had seen a notice of his death, a few moments previous in the paper— oh mother, when I read it, I said, no, no it is not true my Eddie *can't be dead*, no it is *not* so I *could not* believe it, until I got your letter. . . . my own heart is breaking, and I cannot offer you consolation that I would, now, but mother, I *will* pray for you, and for myself, that I may be able to comfort you— Mr R [Annie's husband] begs that you will come on here, soon as you can, and stay with us long as you please—Do dear mother, gather up *all his papers and books,* and take them and come to your own Annie."

onlooker, J. Alden Weston, recalled his impressions: "The burial ceremony, which did not occupy more than three minutes, was so cold-blooded and unchristianlike as to provoke on my part a sense of anger difficult to suppress."[106]

Poe's death notice in the *Baltimore Clipper* on October 9 reported that he died of congestion of the brain. His first obituary, written by Rufus Griswold under the pseudonym of "Ludwig" began, "Edgar Allan Poe is dead. He died in Baltimore the day before yesterday. This announcement will startle many, but few will be grieved by it."[107] Griswold carried out his duties of publishing Poe's works, but his "deliberate distortions," writes editor Eric W. Carlson, in *The Recognition of Edgar Allan Poe*, "in spite of the efforts of Poe's friends to come to his defense, blackened Poe's reputation as a man and a writer here and abroad for decades to come."[108]

Curiously, Poe (pictured) entrusted Rufus Griswold with the posthumous publication of his works. Not only did Griswold write in Poe's obituary that few people would be grieved by the poet's death, but he went on to damage the writer's reputation for many years.

A Writer for the Twenty-First Century

The question of how Poe died is intriguing, but more important is his lasting and widespread impact on literature, both in the United States and abroad. His reputation is assured, not only by the many critics and literary analysts, but also by his popularity among readers of every age.

Edgar Allan Poe's tales and poems continue to be popular. His characters' morbid fascination with death and disease, his themes of guilt and revenge, obsession and insanity, his way with words and hypnotic moods draw critics and readers alike to his works. It is entirely believable that Edgar Allan Poe will influence and inspire writers of poetry, fiction, and criticism for generations to come.

Notes

Chapter 1: A Classical Education

1. Quoted in Dwight Thomas and David K. Jackson, *The Poe Log: A Documentary Life of Edgar Allan Poe 1809–1849*, Boston: G. K. Hall & Co., 1987, p. 9.

2. Vincent Buranelli, *Edgar Allan Poe*, Boston: Twayne Publishers, 1977, p. 35.

3. Quoted in Arthur Hobson Quinn, *Edgar Allan Poe: A Critical Biography*, New York: Appleton/Century, 1941, p. 62.

4. Quoted in Thomas and Jackson, *The Poe Log*, p. 26.

5. Quoted in Quinn, *Edgar Allan Poe: A Critical Biography*, p. 77.

6. Edgar Allan Poe, *The Complete Poems of Edgar Allan Poe*, edited by J. H. Whitty, 1911, reprint, Boston: Houghton Mifflin Company, 1919, p. xxiii.

7. Jeffrey Meyers, "Edgar Allan Poe," in *The Columbia History of American Poetry*, New York: Columbia University Press, 1993, p. 172.

8. Hervey Allen, ed., "Introduction," in Edgar Allan Poe, *Selected Tales and Poems: Edgar Allan Poe, with a Biographical Introduction by Hervey Allen*, 1927, reprint, Roslyn, NY: Walter J. Black, Inc., 1943, p. iii.

9. Quoted in Edward Wagenknecht, *Edgar Allan Poe: The Man Behind the Legend*, New York: Oxford University Press, 1963, p. 16.

10. Quoted in Wagenknecht, *Edgar Allan Poe: The Man Behind the Legend*, p. 16.

11. J. H. Whitty, "Memoir," in Poe, *Complete Poems*, p. xxv.

12. Poe, *Complete Poems*, p. 120.

13. Buranelli, *Edgar Allan Poe*, p. 35.

14. Quoted in Quinn, *Edgar Allan Poe: A Critical Biography*, p. 89.

15. Quoted in Quinn, *Edgar Allan Poe: A Critical Biography*, p. 91.

Chapter 2: Cast upon a Sea of Troubles

16. Edgar Allan Poe, *Letters of Edgar Allan Poe*, edited by John Ward Ostrom, Cambridge, MA: Harvard University Press, 1948, p. 6.

17. William Bittner, *Poe: A Biography*, Boston: Little, Brown & Company, 1962, pp. 45–46.

18. Quoted in Thomas and Jackson, *The Poe Log*, p. 74.

19. Quoted in Thomas and Jackson, *The Poe Log*, p. 74.

20. Poe, *Letters*, p. 7.

21. Poe, *Letters*, pp. 7–8.

22. Poe, *Letters*, p. 8.

23. Quoted in Thomas and Jackson, *The Poe Log*, p. 78.

24. Allen, "Introduction," in Poe, *Selected Tales and Poems*, p. vii.

25. Poe, *Letters*, pp. 10–11.

26. Allen, "Introduction," in Poe, *Selected Tales and Poems*, pp. vii–viii.

27. Poe, *Letters*, pp. 16–17.

28. Poe, *Letters*, p. 19.

29. Quoted in Thomas and Jackson, *The Poe Log*, p. 103.

30. Quoted in Bill Kauffman, "Of Poe and Lee and Other West Points," *American Enterprise*, July 1999, p. 78.

31. Poe, *Letters*, pp. 43–44.

32. Poe, *Letters*, p. 47.

Chapter 3: Richmond Journalist and Family Man

33. Quoted in Thomas and Jackson, *The Poe Log*, pp. 133–34.

34. Quoted in Thomas and Jackson, *The Poe Log*, p. 137.

35. Poe, *Letters*, p. 63.

36. Bittner, *Poe: A Biography*, pp. 106–107.

37. Quoted in Thomas and Jackson, *The Poe Log*, pp. 171–72.

38. Quoted in Thomas and Jackson, *The Poe Log*, p. 173.

39. Bittner, *Poe: A Biography*, p. 111.

40. Paul Lewis, "Poe's Humor: A Psychological Analysis," *Studies in Short Fiction*, Fall 1989, p. 539.

41. Bittner, *Poe: A Biography*, p. 123.

Chapter 4: "Coining One's Brain to Silver"

42. Quoted in Thomas Woodson, ed., *Twentieth-Century Interpretations of "The Fall of the House of Usher,"* Englewood Cliffs, NJ: Prentice-Hall, Inc., 1969, p. 9.

43. George E. Woodberry, *Edgar Allan Poe*, Boston: Houghton Mifflin Company, 1885, p. 120.

44. Quoted in Woodberry, *Edgar Allan Poe*, p. 117.

45. James A. Harrison, *The Complete Works of Edgar Allan Poe*, vol. 1, *Biography*, New York: Thomas Y. Crowell & Co., 1902, pp. 147–48.

46. Quoted in Thomas and Jackson, *The Poe Log*, p. 299.

47. Poe, *Letters*, p. 140.

48. Poe, *Letters*, p. 150.

49. Bittner, *Poe: A Biography*, p. 152.

50. Quoted in Harrison, *The Complete Works of Edgar Allan Poe*, p. 139.

51. Poe, *Letters*, pp. 175–76.

52. Poe, *Letters*, p. 172.

53. Poe, *Letters*, p. 328.

54. John H. Ingram, *Edgar Allan Poe: His Life, Letters, and Opinions*, 2 vols., London: John Hogg, 1880, pp. 182–83.

Chapter 5: Tragedy Strikes and Stays

55. Hervey Allen, *Israfel: The Life and Times of Edgar Allan Poe*, New York: Farrar & Rinehart, Inc., 1934, pp. 403–404.

56. Allen, *Israfel*, pp. 417–18.

57. Allen, *Israfel*, p. 432.

58. Allen, *Israfel*, p. 426.

59. Poe, *Letters*, p. 197.

60. Bittner, *Edgar Allan Poe*, pp. 176–77.

61. Allen, *Israfel*, p. 431.

62. Poe, *Letters*, p. 211.

63. Quoted in J. H. Whitty, "Memoir," in Poe, *Complete Poems*, pp. xliii–xliv.

64. Quoted in Thomas and Jackson, *The Poe Log*, p. 387.

65. Edgar Allan Poe, *Collected Works of Edgar Allan Poe: Poems*, edited by Thomas Ollive Mabbott, Cambridge, MA: Harvard University Press, Belknap Press, 1969, pp. 325–26.

66. Poe, *Letters*, p. 229.

67. Poe, *Letters*, p. 229.

68. Quoted in Poe, *Letters*, p. 245.

69. Quoted in Thomas and Jackson, *The Poe Log*, p. 451.

70. Quinn, *Edgar Allan Poe: A Critical Biography*, p. 404.

Chapter 6: The Depths and the Heights

71. Quoted in Allen, *Israfel*, p. 495.

72. Quinn, *Edgar Allan Poe: A Critical Biography*, p. 439.

73. Allen, *Israfel*, p. 508.

74. Quoted in Jeffrey Meyers, *Edgar Allan Poe: His Life and Legacy*, New York: Charles Scribner's Sons, 1992, p. 172.

75. Meyers, *Poe: His Life and Legacy*, p. 172.

76. Meyers, *Poe: His Life and Legacy*, p. 171.

77. Quoted in Thomas and Jackson, *The Poe Log*, p. 641.

78. John Ward Ostrom, "Edgar A. Poe: His Income as a Literary Entrepreneur," *Poe Studies,* June 1982, p. 5.

79. Quoted in Thomas and Jackson, *The Poe Log,* p. 615.

Chapter 7: Personal Cost

80. Poe, *Letters,* pp. 325–26.

81. Poe, *Letters,* p. 326.

82. Quoted in Thomas and Jackson, *The Poe Log,* p. 668.

83. Quoted in Poe, *Letters,* p. 339.

84. Quoted in Quinn, *Edgar Allan Poe: A Critical Biography,* p. 527.

85. Quoted in Quinn, *Edgar Allan Poe: A Critical Biography,* p. 528.

86. Quoted in Quinn, *Edgar Allan Poe: A Critical Biography,* p. 530.

87. Quoted in Edgar Allan Poe, "The American Drama," in *Essays and Reviews,* New York: Literary Classics of the United States, Inc., 1984, pp. 366–67.

88. Quoted in Thomas and Jackson, *The Poe Log,* p. 714.

89. Quoted in Thomas and Jackson, *The Poe Log,* p. 742.

90. Quoted in Thomas and Jackson, *The Poe Log,* p. 741.

Chapter 8: A Mysterious Death

91. Poe, *Collected Works: Poems,* p. 461.

92. Poe, *Letters,* p. 433.

93. Poe, *Letters,* p. 452.

94. Quoted in Poe, *Collected Works: Poems,* p. 567.

95. Quoted in Thomas and Jackson, *The Poe Log,* p. 839.

96. Poe, *Letters,* p. 461.

97. Quoted in Quinn, *Edgar Allan Poe: A Critical Biography,* p. 636.

98. Quoted in Thomas and Jackson, *The Poe Log,* p. 843.

99. Quoted in John Evangelist Walsh, *Midnight Dreary: The Mysterious Death of Edgar Allan Poe,* New Brunswick, NJ: Rutgers University Press, 1998, pp. 71–72.

100. Quoted in Thomas and Jackson, *The Poe Log,* p. 844.

101. Quoted in Thomas and Jackson, *The Poe Log,* p. 845.

102. Quoted in Walsh, *Midnight Dreary,* p. 42.

103. John J. Moran, "Letter to Mrs. Clemm," quoted in Thomas and Jackson, *The Poe Log,* p. 846.

104. Quoted in Thomas and Jackson, *The Poe Log,* p. 846.

105. Quoted in Thomas and Jackson, *The Poe Log,* p. 848.

106. Quoted in Thomas and Jackson, *The Poe Log,* p. 848.

107. Rufus Wilmot Griswold, "The 'Ludwig' Article," in Eric W. Carlson, ed., *The Recognition of Edgar Allan Poe,* Ann Arbor: University of Michigan Press, 1966, p. 29.

108. Carlson, *The Recognition of Edgar Allan Poe,* p. 29.

For Further Reading

Madelyn Klein Anderson, *Edgar Allan Poe: A Mystery*. New York: Franklin Watts, 1993. A well-researched work that features many quotations with the author's explanations and interpretations.

Lettice Ulpha Cooper, *The Young Edgar Allan Poe*. London: Max Parrish, 1964. Fictionized but based on extensive research, this readable biography covers Poe's first eighteen years, followed by a brief epilogue on his adult life.

Charles Haines, *Edgar Allan Poe: His Writings and Influence*. New York: Franklin Watts, 1974. Haines weaves many interpretations of Poe's works and letters into his biography.

William Jay Jacobs, *Edgar Allan Poe: Genius in Torment*. New York: McGraw-Hill, 1975. Set in Poe's historical background, this readable biography interprets Poe's life as an author.

Suzanne LeVert, *Edgar Allan Poe*. New York: Chelsea House, 1992. This biography emphasizes the way Poe's strange themes mirror his life.

Nancy Loewen, *Poe: A Biography*. Mankato, MN: Creative Editions, 1993. A picture book whose photos by Tina Mucci provide mood and context for excerpts from Poe's works.

Russell Shorto, *Edgar Allan Poe: Creator of Dreams*. New York: Kipling Press, 1988. A sympathetic biography that emphasizes psychological aspects of Poe's writing.

Bonnie Szumski, Ed., *Readings on Edgar Allan Poe*. San Diego, CA: Greenhaven Press, Inc., 1998. Eighteen essays evaluating Poe as a writer, analyzing his themes, and proposing a variety of approaches to his tales, including Poe's own discussion of his poem "The Raven."

Philip Van Doren Stern, *Edgar Allan Poe, Visitor From the Night of Time*. New York: Thomas Y. Crowell, 1973. This interpretive study is based on Poe's letters as well as on critical studies of his works, many of which considered his writings to be autobiographical.

Works Consulted

Books

Hervey Allen, *Israfel: The Life and Times of Edgar Allan Poe.* New York: Farrar & Rinehart, Inc., 1934. Reissue, with corrections, of the earlier two-volume Poe biography published in 1926. Gives extensive attention to intellectual and physical background of Poe's life and times.

Hervey Allen and Thomas Ollive Mabbott, *Poe's Brother: The Poems of William Henry Leonard Poe.* New York: George H. Doran Company, 1926. Presents documentation on the relationship between the Poe brothers and facsimiles of letters and publications.

Margaret Alterton, *Origins of Poe's Critical Theory,* Vol. ii, no. 3, Iowa City: University of Iowa Humanistic Studies, 1925. This extended scholarly study contains detailed comments on the writings familiar to Poe and the relationship between ideas and passages in these works and in his works.

William Bittner, *Poe: A Biography.* Boston: Little, Brown & Company, 1962. Readable study that rounds out the study of Poe by reviewing both favorable and unfavorable accounts of his life and works.

Vincent Buranelli, *Edgar Allan Poe.* Boston: Twayne Publishers, 1977. Analysis of Poe's works and literary reputation.

Eric W. Carlson, ed., *The Recognition of Edgar Allan Poe.* Ann Arbor: University of Michigan Press, 1966. Collection of contemporaneous notices and reviews of Poe's works followed by critical articles from 1850 to 1963.

Thomas Holley Chivers, *Life of Poe.* Edited with an introduction by Richard Beale Davis. New York: E. P. Dutton & Co., Inc., 1952. Account by personal acquaintance of Poe.

Michael J. Deas, *The Portraits and Daguerreotypes of Edgar Allan Poe.* Charlottesville: University Press of Virginia, 1988. Well-illustrated discussion of the many likenesses of Poe and histories of their whereabouts throughout the years.

James A. Harrison, *The Complete Works of Edgar Allan Poe.* Vol. 1: *Biography.* New York: Thomas Y. Crowell & Co., 1902. Harrison's research was enhanced by recollections of some of the people who had known Poe personally.

George Egon Hatvary, *Horace Binney Wallace.* Boston: G. K. Hall & Co., 1977. Explores the relationship between Poe and two of his literary friends, Rufus Griswold and Horace Binney Wallace.

John H. Ingram, *Edgar Allan Poe: His Life, Letters, and Opinions.* 2 vols. London: John Hogg, 1880. Developed from Ingram's extensive collection of letters from people who knew Poe personally.

Joseph Wood Krutch, *Edgar Allan Poe: A Study in Genius.* 1929. Reprint, New York: Russell & Russell, 1965. Tries to show that Poe's genius arose from and was dependent on a disordered personality. Many interesting visual likenesses of Poe.

A. Robert Lee, *Edgar Allan Poe: The Design of Order.* London: Vision Press Limited, 1987. Essays that focus on the unity that permeates Poe's life and works.

Dumas Malone, *Jefferson and His Time: The Sage of Monticello.* Boston: Little, Brown & Company, 1981. Vol. 5 in Malone's biography of Thomas Jefferson gives extensive account of the University of Virginia.

Charles E. May, *Edgar Allan Poe: A Study of the Short Fiction.* Boston: Twayne Publishers, 1991. Analyzes Poe's short stories to show how they contributed to the development of the modern short story as an art form.

Tara McCarthy, *Teaching the Stories and Poems of Edgar Allan Poe.* New York: Scholastic, Inc., 1999. Synopses, pre-reading activities, outlines for class discussions, readers' theater, and other ideas for teachers and classroom learning.

Jeffrey Meyers, *Edgar Allan Poe: His Life and Legacy.* New York: Charles Scribner's Sons, 1992. Probes the development of Poe's heart and mind, his nature as a man and a poet. Highly interpretive.

Jeffrey Meyers, "Edgar Allan Poe," in *The Columbia History of American Poetry.* Jay Parini, ed. New York: Columbia University Press, 1993. Comprehensive overview of Poe as a poet.

John J. Moran, M.D., *A Defense of Edgar Allan Poe: Life, Character, and Dying Declarations of the Poet.* Washington, DC: William F. Boogher, Publisher, 1885. A largely discredited account of Poe's death by the physician who attended him at the time.

Jay Parini, ed., *The Columbia History of American Poetry.* New York: Columbia University Press, 1993. Essays on the entire roster of prominent American poets from the seventeenth century to the present.

Edgar Allan Poe, *Collected Works of Edgar Allan Poe: Poems.* Edited by Thomas Ollive Mabbott. Cambridge, MA: Harvard University Press, Belknap Press, 1969. Contains extensive notes on the poems.

Edgar Allan Poe, *Collected Works of Edgar Allan Poe: Tales and Sketches.* Edited by Thomas Ollive Mabbott. Cambridge, MA: Harvard University Press, Belknap Press, 1978. The completion of Mabbott's three-volume compendium of Poe's works, which includes the author's prose but none of his critical essays.

Edgar Allan Poe, *The Complete Poems of Edgar Allan Poe.* Edited by J. H. Whitty. 1911. Reprint, Boston: Houghton Mifflin Company, 1919. Whitty's "Memoir" on the life of Poe provides several interviews and references not included in other biographies.

Edgar Allan Poe, *Essays and Reviews.* New York: Literary Classics of the United States, Inc., 1984. A large collection of

Poe's critical works with notes by G. R. Thompson. Interesting reading for students interested in Poe's times.

Edgar Allan Poe, *The Last Letters of Edgar Allan Poe to Sarah Helen Whitman.* Edited by James A. Harrison. New York: G. P. Putnam's Sons, 1909. Poe's letters to Whitman.

Edgar Allan Poe, *The Letters of Edgar Allan Poe.* Edited by John Ward Ostrom. Cambridge, MA: Harvard University Press, 1948. Two-volume collection of Poe's letters with detailed notes on the persons and events mentioned.

Edgar Allan Poe, *Poetry and Tales.* New York: Viking Press, 1984. Composite of texts copyrighted earlier and appearing with notes by Patrick F. Quinn, this volume is a comprehensive collection of Poe's poetry and stories.

Edgar Allan Poe, *Selected Tales and Poems: Edgar Allan Poe, with a Biographical Introduction by Hervey Allen.* 1927. Reprint, Roslyn, NY: Walter J. Black, Inc., 1943. Allen's short biography includes some of the newest scholarship available at the time he wrote the original in 1927.

Edgar Allan Poe, *The Works of Edgar Allan Poe.* New York: A. C. Armstrong & Son, 1876. Contains selected poems, essays, tales, and marginal notes by Poe. Appendices include documents read at the establishment of the Poe Memorial in Baltimore in 1876.

Arthur Hobson Quinn, *Edgar Allan Poe: A Critical Biography.* New York: Appleton/Century, 1941. This careful and extensive study by Quinn of all documents available to him gives a balanced and positive picture of Poe.

Arthur Hobson Quinn and Richard H. Hart, *Edgar Allan Poe: Letters and Documents in the Enoch Pratt Free Library.* New York: Scholars' Facsimiles & Reprints, 1941. Reproductions, with notes, of letters to and about Poe.

Patrick F. Quinn, *The French Face of Edgar Poe.* Carbondale: Southern Illinois University Press, 1957. Commentary on studies made of Edgar Allan Poe and his works by French critics, especially poet Charles A. Baudelaire.

Amanda Pogue Schulte, *Facts About Poe: Portraits and Daguerreotypes of Edgar Allan Poe.* Charlottesville: University of Virginia, 1926. Schulte studies the authenticity of visual likenesses of Poe, giving explanatory notes.

Kenneth Silverman, ed., *New Essays on Poe's Major Tales.* New York: Cambridge University Press, 1993. Highly speculative psychological interpretations of Poe.

Dwight Thomas and David K. Jackson, *The Poe Log: A Documentary Life of Edgar Allan Poe, 1809–1849.* Boston: G. K. Hall & Co., 1987. Date by date account of events in Poe's life.

Edward Wagenknecht, *Edgar Allan Poe: The Man Behind the Legend.* New York: Oxford University Press, 1963. Focuses on the character and personality of Poe; gives only incidental concern to Poe's works.

John Evangelist Walsh, *Midnight Dreary: The Mysterious Death of Edgar Allan Poe.* New Brunswick, NJ: Rutgers University Press, 1998. Walsh reviews old and new evidence to present a fresh account of the last month of Poe's life.

John Evangelist Walsh, *Poe the Detective: The Curious Circumstances Behind "The Mystery of Marie Roget."* New Brunswick, NJ: Rutgers University Press, 1968. The text of Poe's story, "The Mystery of Marie Roget" and the facts known about the murder of Mary Rogers, with speculations on the relationship between the two stories.

Frances Winwar, *The Haunted Palace: A Life of Edgar Allan Poe.* New York: Harper, 1959. Study of the relationship of Poe's life and personality to his works, with special attention for the women in his life.

George E. Woodberry, *Edgar Allan Poe.* Boston: Houghton Mifflin Company, 1885. One of the earlier studies of Poe's life and works.

Thomas Woodson, ed., *Twentieth-Century Interpretations of "The Fall of the House of Usher."* Englewood Cliffs: Prentice-Hall, Inc., 1969. Exhaustive variety of discussions on Poe's most finely crafted tale.

Periodicals

Thomas C. Carlson, "Biographical Warfare: Silent Film and the Public Image of Poe," *Mississippi Quarterly,* Winter 1998.

William Connery, "The Mysterious Death of E. A. Poe," *World & I,* October 1999.

William Connery, "The Poe Society," *World & I,* October 1999.

Joseph Costa, "A 39-Year-Old Man With Mental Status Change," *Maryland Medical Journal,* September 1996.

Jerome DeNuccio, "History, Narrative, and Authority: Poe's Literary Analysis of Poe's First-Published Tale, 'Metzengterstein,'" *College Literature,* June 1997.

George Egon Hatvary, "Poe's Borrowings from H. B. Wallace," *American Literature,* November 1976.

Kevin J. Hayes, "Poe's Earliest Reading," *English Language Notes,* March 1995.

Bill Kauffman, "Of Poe and Lee and Other West Points," *American Enterprise,* July 1999.

Paul Lewis, "Poe's Humor: A Psychological Analysis," *Studies in Short Fiction,* Fall 1989.

John Ward Ostrom, "Edgar A. Poe: His Income as a Literary Entrepreneur," *Poe Studies,* June 1982.

Judith E. Pike, "Poe and the Revenge of the Exquisite Corpse," *Studies in American Fiction,* Autumn 1992.

Burton R. Pollin, "Maria Clemm, Poe's Aunt: His Boon or His Bane?" *Mississippi Quarterly,* Spring 1995.

Burton R. Pollin, "Poe 'Viewed and Reviewed': An Annotated Checklist of Contemporaneous Notices," *Poe Studies,* December 1980.

Anne Revis, "Mr. Jefferson's Charlottesville," *National Geographic Magazine,* May 1950.

Kate E. Stewart, "An Early Imitative Ape: A Possible Source for 'The Murders in the Rue Morgue,'" *Poe Studies*, June 1987.

Susan Archer Weiss, "The Last Days of Edgar A. Poe," *Scribner's Monthly*, May 1878.

Terence Whalen, "Poe's 'Diddling' and the Depression: Notes on the Sources of Swindling," *Studies in American Fiction*, Autumn 1995.

Internet Sources

The Poe Museum in Baltimore, Maryland, http://www.eapoe.org.

The Poe Museum, 1914–16, East Main St., Richmond, VA 23223, http://www.edgar allanpoemuseum@erols.com.

Index

Picture Credits

Cover photo: Flavius Fisher/Valentine Museum

© Bettmann/Corbis, 54, 73, 74, 81, 108

Brown Brothers, 13, 35, 40, 45, 65, 71

© Corbis, 30, 31

Culver Pictures, 15, 16, 51, 53, 78, 83, 99

Dictionary of American Portraits, Dover Publications, Inc., 27, 33, 56, 67, 91, 94, 103

FPG International, 10

Giraudon/Art Resource, NY, 68

Hulton Getty Collection/Archive Photos, 21

Image Select/Art Resource, NY, 61

Library of Congress, 24, 47, 75, 88

MPI/Archive Photos, 43

Prints Old and Rare, 97

SEF/Art Resource, NY, 26

Smithsonian American Art Museum, Washington, DC/Art Resource, NY, 59

© Lee Snider/Corbis, 106

About the Author

Rafael Tilton is an educator, editor, and writer who has written six other books for young people. Tilton's interest in short stories, poetry, and detective fiction grows out of a career spent teaching literature and writing in high school and college classrooms.

THE
CATAWBAS

THE
CATAWBAS

James H. Merrell
Vassar College

Frank W. Porter III
General Editor

CHELSEA HOUSE PUBLISHERS
New York   Philadelphia

On the cover Catawba vase with
Indian head handles made
by Sara Ayers in 1979.

Chelsea House Publishers
Editor-in-Chief Nancy Toff
Executive Editor Remmel T. Nunn
Managing Editor Karyn Gullen Browne
Copy Chief Juliann Barbato
Picture Editor Adrian G. Allen
Art Director Maria Epes
Manufacturing Manager Gerald Levine

Indians of North America
Senior Editor Marjorie P. K. Weiser

Staff for **THE CATAWBAS**
Assistant Editor Karen Schimmel
Deputy Copy Chief Ellen Scordato
Editorial Assistant Clark Morgan
Assistant Art Director Laurie Jewell
Designer Ghila Krajzman
Picture Researcher Lynn Goldberg Biderman
Production Coordinator Joseph Romano

7 9 8 6

Library of Congress Cataloging in Publication Data

Merrell, James Hart, 1953–
The Catawbas / James H. Merrell.
   p. cm.—(Indians of North America)
ISBN 1-55546-694-X
    0-7910-0356-6 (pbk.)

1. Catawba Indians. I. Title. II. Series: Indians of North
America (Chelsea House Publishers)
E99.C24M47 1989   88-21821
973'.0497—dc 19   CIP

CONTENTS

INDIANS OF NORTH AMERICA

CHELSEA HOUSE PUBLISHERS

INDIANS OF NORTH AMERICA: CONFLICT AND SURVIVAL

Frank W. Porter III

The Indians survived our open intention of wiping them out, and since the tide turned they have even weathered our good intentions toward them, which can be much more deadly.

John Steinbeck
America and Americans

When Europeans first reached the North American continent, they found hundreds of tribes occupying a vast and rich country. The newcomers quickly recognized the wealth of natural resources. They were not, however, so quick or willing to recognize the spiritual, cultural, and intellectual riches of the people they called Indians.

The Indians of North America examines the problems that develop when people with different cultures come together. For American Indians, the consequences of their interaction with non-Indian people have been both productive and tragic. The Europeans believed they had "discovered" a "New World," but their religious bigotry, cultural bias, and materialistic world view kept them from appreciating and understanding the people who lived in it. All too often they attempted to change the way of life of the indigenous people. The Spanish conquistadores wanted the Indians as a source of labor. The Christian missionaries, many of whom were English, viewed them as potential converts. French traders and trappers used the Indians as a means to obtain pelts. As Francis Parkman, the 19th-century historian, stated, "Spanish civilization crushed the Indian; English civilization scorned and neglected him; French civilization embraced and cherished him."

Nearly 500 years later, many people think of American Indians as curious vestiges of a distant past, waging a futile war to survive in a Space Age society. Even today, our understanding of the history and culture of American Indians is too often derived from unsympathetic, culturally biased, and inaccurate reports. The American Indian, described and portrayed in thousands of movies, television programs, books, articles, and government studies, has either been raised to the status of the "noble savage" or disparaged as the "wild Indian" who resisted the westward expansion of the American frontier.

7

Where in this popular view are the real Indians, the human beings and communities whose ancestors can be traced back to ice-age hunters? Where are the creative and indomitable people whose sophisticated technologies used the natural resources to ensure their survival, whose military skill might even have prevented European settlement of North America if not for devastating epidemics and the disruption of the ecology? Where are the men and women who are today diligently struggling to assert their legal rights and express once again the value of their heritage?

The various Indian tribes of North America, like people everywhere, have a history that includes population expansion, adaptation to a range of regional environments, trade across wide networks, internal strife, and warfare. This was the reality. Europeans justified their conquests, however, by creating a mythical image of the New World and its native people. In this myth, the New World was a virgin land, waiting for the Europeans. The arrival of Christopher Columbus ended a timeless primitiveness for the original inhabitants.

Also part of this myth was the debate over the origins of the American Indians. Fantastic and diverse answers were proposed by the early explorers, missionaries, and settlers. Some thought that the Indians were descended from the Ten Lost Tribes of Israel, others that they were descended from inhabitants of the lost continent of Atlantis. One writer suggested that the Indians had reached North America in another Noah's ark.

A later myth, perpetrated by many historians, focused on the relentless persecution during the past five centuries until only a scattering of these "primitive" people remained to be herded onto reservations. This view fails to chronicle the overt and covert ways in which the Indians successfully coped with the intruders.

All of these myths presented one-sided interpretations that ignored the complexity of European and American events and policies. All left serious questions unanswered. What were the origins of the American Indians? Where did they come from? How and when did they get to the New World? What was their life—their culture—really like?

In the late 1800s, anthropologists and archaeologists in the Smithsonian Institution's newly created Bureau of American Ethnology in Washington, D. C., began to study scientifically the history and culture of the Indians of North America. They were motivated by an honest belief that the Indians were on the verge of extinction and that along with them would vanish their languages, religious beliefs, technology, myths, and legends. These men and women went out to visit, study, and record data from as many Indian communities as possible before this information was forever lost.

8

By this time there was a new myth in the national consciousness. American Indians existed as figures in the American past. They had performed a historical mission. They had challenged white settlers who trekked across the continent. Once conquered, however, they were supposed to accept graciously the way of life of their conquerors.

The reality again was different. American Indians resisted both actively and passively. They refused to lose their unique identity, to be assimilated into white society. Many whites viewed the Indians not only as members of a conquered nation but also as "inferior" and "unequal." The rights of the Indians could be expanded, contracted, or modified as the conquerors saw fit. In every generation, white society asked itself what to do with the American Indians. Their answers have resulted in the twists and turns of federal Indian policy.

There were two general approaches. One way was to raise the Indians to a "higher level" by "civilizing" them. Zealous missionaries considered it their Christian duty to elevate the Indian through conversion and scanty education. The other approach was to ignore the Indians until they disappeared under pressure from the ever-expanding white society. The myth of the "vanishing Indian" gave stronger support to the latter option, helping to justify the taking of the Indians' land.

Prior to the end of the 18th century, there was no national policy on Indians simply because the American nation had not yet come into existence. American Indians similarly did not possess a political or social unity with which to confront the various Europeans. They were not homogeneous. Rather, they were loosely formed bands and tribes, speaking nearly 300 languages and thousands of dialects. The collective identity felt by Indians today is a result of their common experiences of defeat and/or mistreatment at the hands of whites.

During the colonial period, the British crown did not have a coordinated policy toward the Indians of North America. Specific tribes (most notably the Iroquois and the Cherokee) became military and political pawns used by both the crown and the individual colonies. The success of the American Revolution brought no immediate change. When the United States acquired new territory from France and Mexico in the early 19th century, the federal government wanted to open this land to settlement by homesteaders. But the Indian tribes that lived on this land had signed treaties with European governments assuring their title to the land. Now the United States assumed legal responsibility for honoring these treaties.

At first, President Thomas Jefferson believed that the Louisiana Purchase contained sufficient land for both the Indians and the white population.

Within a generation, though, it became clear that the Indians would not be allowed to remain. In the 1830s the federal government began to coerce the eastern tribes to sign treaties agreeing to relinquish their ancestral land and move west of the Mississippi River. Whenever these negotiations failed, President Andrew Jackson used the military to remove the Indians. The southeastern tribes, promised food and transportation during their removal to the West, were instead forced to walk the "Trail of Tears." More than 4,000 men, women, and children died during this forced march. The "removal policy" was successful in opening the land to homesteaders, but it created enormous hardships for the Indians.

By 1871 most of the tribes in the United States had signed treaties ceding most or all of their ancestral land in exchange for reservations and welfare. The treaty terms were intended to bind both parties for all time. But in the General Allotment Act of 1887, the federal government changed its policy again. Now the goal was to make tribal members into individual landowners and farmers, encouraging their absorption into white society. This policy was advantageous to whites who were eager to acquire Indian land, but it proved disastrous for the Indians. One hundred thirty-eight million acres of reservation land were subdivided into tracts of 160, 80, or as little as 40 acres, and allotted to tribe members on an individual basis. Land owned in this way was said to have "trust status" and could not be sold. But the surplus land—all Indian land not allotted to individuals— was opened (for sale) to white settlers. Ultimately, more than 90 million acres of land were taken from the Indians by legal and illegal means.

The resulting loss of land was a catastrophe for the Indians. It was necessary to make it illegal for Indians to sell their land to non-Indians. The Indian Reorganization Act of 1934 officially ended the allotment period. Tribes that voted to accept the provisions of this act were reorganized, and an effort was made to purchase land within preexisting reservations to restore an adequate land base.

Ten years later, in 1944, federal Indian policy again shifted. Now the federal government wanted to get out of the "Indian business." In 1953 an act of Congress named specific tribes whose trust status was to be ended "at the earliest possible time." This new law enabled the United States to end unilaterally, whether the Indians wished it or not, the special status that protected the land in Indian tribal reservations. In the 1950s federal Indian policy was to transfer federal responsibility and jurisdiction to state governments, encourage the physical relocation of Indian peoples from reservations to urban areas, and hasten the termination, or extinction, of tribes.

Between 1954 and 1962 Congress passed specific laws authorizing the termination of more than 100 tribal groups. The stated purpose of the termination policy was to ensure the full and complete integration of Indians into American society. However, there is a less benign way to interpret this legislation. Even as termination was being discussed in Congress, 133 separate bills were introduced to permit the transfer of trust land ownership from Indians to non-Indians.

With the Johnson administration in the 1960s the federal government began to reject termination. In the 1970s yet another Indian policy emerged. Known as "self-determination," it favored keeping the protective role of the federal government while increasing tribal participation in, and control of, important areas of local government. In 1983 President Reagan, in a policy statement on Indian affairs, restated the unique "government to government" relationship of the United States with the Indians. However, federal programs since then have moved toward transferring Indian affairs to individual states, which have long desired to gain control of Indian land and resources.

As long as American Indians retain power, land, and resources that are coveted by the states and the federal government, there will continue to be a "clash of cultures," and the issues will be contested in the courts, Congress, the White House, and even in the international human rights community. To give all Americans a greater comprehension of the issues and conflicts involving American Indians today is a major goal of this series. These issues are not easily understood, nor can these conflicts be readily resolved. The study of North American Indian history and culture is a necessary and important step toward that comprehension. All Americans must learn the history of the relations between the Indians and the federal government, recognize the unique legal status of the Indians, and understand the heritage and cultures of the Indians of North America.

Billy Harris, a Catawba Indian, photographed by Frank G. Speck in 1922. Between 1913 and 1950, Speck, an anthropologist from the University of Pennsylvania, frequently visited the Catawba reservation in South Carolina and was able to observe the Catawbas while they still maintained many aspects of their traditional way of life.

ANCIENT TIMES
AND
CHANGING WAYS

On August 29, 1754, in a cabin near what is now Charlotte, North Carolina, the chief of the Catawba Indian Nation stepped forward to speak to an audience of Indians and British colonists.

> [W]e Expect to live on those Lands we now possess During our Time here, [the chief, Hagler, announced] for when the Great man above made us he also made . . . our forefathers and us of this Colour and Hue (Showing his hands and Breast)[;] he also fixed our forefathers and us here and to Inherit this Land and Ever since we Lived after our manner and fashion.

Hagler also spoke about the European colonists, now neighbors of his people. "Ever since they first Came among us," he said, ". . . we have Lived in a Brotherly love and peace with them . . . and it is our Earnest Desire that [the] Love and Friendship which has so Long remain'd should Ever Continue."

In a few words, the Catawba chief captured the two most important themes in his people's history. The first was their deep attachment to homeland, ancestors, and a distinctive way of life. The second was their desire for peace with the European intruders from across the Atlantic. Throughout their recorded history, Catawbas have sought to balance the lessons passed down from their forefathers—the "manner and fashion" of living that Hagler mentioned—with the expectations of the newcomers.

By the time Hagler spoke, Catawbas had been trying to achieve this balance for more than two centuries. In the spring of 1540 the Spanish explorer Hernando de Soto became the first European to have contact with the Catawbas. He led 600 troops through the southern Piedmont region, the upland belt lying between the Atlantic coastal plain of the eastern United States and the Appalachian Mountains to the west. Twenty-six years later other Spaniards, led by Juan Pardo, followed in de Soto's footsteps. These uninvited Spanish visitors turned out to be impolite guests. De Soto was looking for gold, and he did not hesitate to kidnap

A 1731 French edition of an earlier Spanish account detailing Hernando de Soto's exploration of southeastern North America. De Soto, who traveled through the Piedmont in 1540, was the first European to come into contact with the Catawbas.

Indians if he thought they could lead him to a mine—or to kill them if they refused. Fortunately for the Indians, he swept through the area like a tornado—destructively, but quickly—on his way west. Pardo was more patient: Some of his soldiers built forts and stayed a few years rather than a few weeks. Eventually he, too, wore out his welcome,

and in the early 1570s his troops were driven out of the Piedmont by angry Indian warriors. After Pardo's men retreated, the Spaniards left the Catawbas alone and remained primarily among the Indian tribes south and east of the Catawbas, on the coast of present-day Florida and Georgia.

England, Spain's archrival in the race for a colonial empire, was slow to move into the void created by the Spaniards' retreat. In 1585, English colonists settled on Roanoke Island, off the coast of North Carolina, but the colony mysteriously disappeared a few years later. Their successors, who settled farther north along the James River at Jamestown, Virginia, in 1607, were too worried about surviving in the hot climate and too preoccupied with the powerful Powhatan Indians close at hand to contact the Catawbas, who lived several hundred miles away. It was only after 1650—when the now prosperous and expanding colony of Virginia had destroyed the great Powhatan nation and the transplanted English settlers were beginning to feel more at home in this strange land—that the newcomers began to explore the lands southwest of the James River.

These early Virginia explorers may not have known it, but after 1663 they were trespassing on territory claimed by other English colonists. That year King Charles II granted a huge tract of land, named Carolina, to a group of eight powerful English politicians who called themselves the "True and Absolute Lords and Proprietors of Caro-

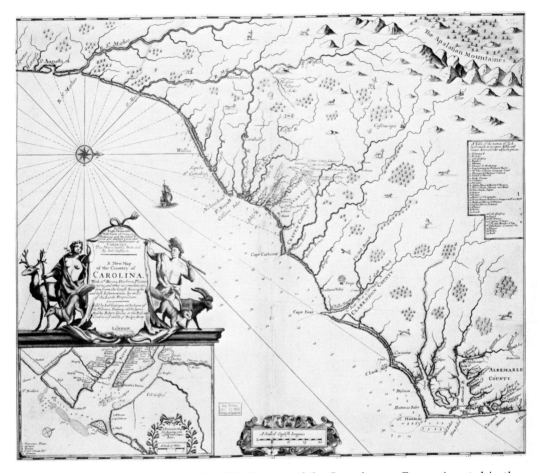

A 1682 map of the colony of Carolina. The location of the Catawbas, or Esaws, is noted in the upper right corner of the map.

lina." The territory promised by the King's charter included most of what are now the states of North Carolina, South Carolina, and Georgia, and extended from the Atlantic Ocean to the "South Seas" (Pacific Ocean). It was designed to serve as protection against England's Spanish enemies in Florida and at the same time make money for its "Lords and Proprietors." At first it did neither, as settlement after settlement failed. Finally, in 1670, a band of colonists founded Charles Town, now Charleston, South Carolina. Within a few years the English were traveling to the Catawba villages 250 miles to the northwest to meet with the Indians. The days of "Brotherly love and peace" that Hagler would speak of in 1754 had begun.

A closer look at Catawba history reveals that Hagler exaggerated a little as he addressed the crowd that August day. For one thing, relations between his people and English colonists had not always been as friendly as he claimed. For another, by 1754 the Catawbas were not really living in a "manner and fashion" that their ancestors would have recognized as their own. Much had changed since Hernando de Soto had first come into contact with them more than 200 years earlier. In trying to combine past and present, familiar ways with foreign imports, the Catawbas stumbled now and then and lost their balance as they listened both to their ancestors and to their new neighbors.

As history shows, this balance was not easy for American Indians to achieve. By Hagler's time many eastern Indian tribes already had toppled in one way or another. Some, heeding the call of the past, had refused to accept the European invasion of their lands, risen in rebellion, and lost both their lands and many lives. Others, listening to the voice of the new more than the old, embraced the ways of the foreigner and disappeared as a distinct people, losing their Indian identity as they tried to be more like the English. Catawbas, though they squabbled with colonists on occasion and altered their customs as times changed, never fell into either of these traps. They kept their balance and survived when so many other Indians did not. To understand how the Catawbas overcame the odds and en-

dured, we must first go back to the remote past, before Hagler, before Carolina, before de Soto—even before "Catawba."

Much is known about the European colonists who came to North America during the past few hundred years, but very little is certain about the first people who arrived on this continent thousands of years before that. What is known about these ancient human beings is the result of archaeology, the scientific study of the material remains of past societies. Archaeologists dig into the earth with great care to uncover what people left behind, and they use what they find—from arrowheads and clay pots to fireplaces and postholes; from skeletons and seeds to necklaces and even garbage—to reconstruct the way people lived in the past.

Archaeologists are not certain just how long ago the first people arrived in North America. Most archaeologists today believe that the first Americans arrived somewhere between 25,000 and 12,000 years before the present (B.P.), and that they came from northern Asia. There is more certainty about how the newcomers got here: They walked. Although it would be impossible to do so today, it was relatively easy 12,000 years ago. At that time the world was in the late Pleistocene, the last Ice Age. The climate was much colder than it is today, and glaciers covered much of North America. These huge sheets of ice contained so much of the earth's supply of water that sea levels were significantly lower than they are today. As a result, land that is now under water was dry. At that time a land bridge connected Asia and North America. It was across this land bridge, which today is submerged beneath the Bering Strait separating Russia and Alaska, that the first human beings entered North America.

These first settlers, whom scholars call Paleo-Indians (paleo- means "ancient"), did not think of themselves as colonists. They were big-game hunters, and they came to America on the trail of their prey—the mammoth, the great bison, and other large beasts. These animals are all extinct today but were then a major source of food. Although the Paleo-Indians also relied on small game such as rabbits, their lives depended on slaying the huge creatures that roamed the land during the last Ice Age. As a result, their entire way of life was oriented around the hunt. They lived in small bands, frequently moving from place to place in search of game. When they did settle down, they chose campsites in the hills, where the animals they hunted were most likely to be found.

To kill their prey the Paleo-Indians used weapons with stone tips, which archaeologists call projectile points. They shaped the points by chipping away flakes of rock until the stones had a sharp edge. The points were attached to a bone or wood shaft to make a spear for throwing or thrusting into an animal. Once a mammoth or great bison was slain, the entire band set to work. Any meat that was not eaten on the spot was dried for later use. The skin and

These stone scrapers, uncovered at the Hardaway Site near Badin, North Carolina, are the earliest stone tools found in the North Carolina Piedmont region. They date from the Paleo-Indian period, 12,000 to 10,000 years ago.

hair were made into clothing, and the bones became tools. Nothing was wasted.

Over several thousand years, Paleo-Indians and their big-game hunting ways spread throughout North America. Game was plentiful, and the Indian population increased. At some time between 12,000 and 10,000 years ago some Paleo-Indians followed the game to the Yadkin River valley in central North Carolina, just east of the area that Europeans later called "Catawba Country." They climbed a hill that overlooked the river, made a crude fireplace out of stones, and built the first of many fires in the area. This site, named the Hardaway Site after the construction company that was at one time located there, is the first known residence of Paleo-Indian people in the southern Piedmont.

There is plenty of evidence that the Hardaway people were not alone in the region. Many other projectile points that are believed to date from these times have been found scattered throughout the Piedmont. Unfortunately, because the hunting bands never stayed for long in one place, they left few traces of their way of life. For this reason, it is difficult for archaeologists to pinpoint other Paleo-Indian sites in the area and learn more about the lives of these people. These big-game hunters, however, were probably much like the Paleo-Indians in other parts of North America during the last Ice Age.

After about 10,000 B.P. the Paleo-Indians of the southern Piedmont, like their contemporaries elsewhere in

Polished stone tools dating from the Archaic period, 10,000 to 3,000 years ago.

North America, experienced dramatic changes. As the Ice Age ended and the glaciers retreated, the big game that had flourished in the colder climate died out, their extinction perhaps hastened by the skills of Paleo-Indian hunters. During the years that followed, known as the Archaic period (which lasted from about 10,000 to 3,000 B.P. in most of North America), the descendants of these successful hunters had to cope with very different conditions. Regions that were once grasslands now became forests, and the melting glaciers formed rivers and lakes. This new environment was very similar to our own environment today.

The Indians of the Archaic period did not change their way of life overnight, nor did they completely abandon the customs of their ancestors. Rather, Archaic Indian life developed gradually out of Paleo-Indian culture. The two used many of the same types of tools, lived in small family groups, relied heavily on hunting, and moved frequently from one site to another. Over the course of time, however, the Archaic Indians developed a culture that was truly their own. They still obtained much of their food through hunting— although for deer, not the great bison or woolly mammoth—but they now supplemented their diet by fishing and gathering foods that grew wild in the environment. More diverse plant foods such as seeds, berries, nuts, leaves, and roots grew well in the warmer climate that evolved during the Archaic period. The invention of a wider array of spe-

The atlatl, or spear thrower, increased the force with which a hunter could throw a spear. Its appearance during the Archaic period helped distinguish Archaic culture from the earlier Paleo-Indian culture.

cialized tools, in particular bone hooks for catching fish, mortars for grinding seeds and nuts, and the atlatl, or spear-thrower (a device that increased the force with which a hunter could throw a spear), made obtaining food much easier. Many tools were now made of polished rather than chipped stone. Polishing improved the efficiency of some tools. For example, it was easier to grind seeds to fine meal with polished milling stones than with rough-surfaced chipped ones. To further increase their efficiency Indians became more sedentary, more tied to a specific locality within an area. They still moved about from season to season to hunt and collect food, but over time familiarity with a particular territory enabled Indians to know where food was most likely to be—where the nuts and berries

A pottery container restored from fragments uncovered at the Hardaway Site in North Carolina. The pattern on the vessel was made by pressing a piece of hide against the wet clay.

were thickest on the ground, where fish could best be caught and deer most easily be killed.

With improved tools the Indians became better at hunting and gathering. As a result, they had time to devote to other pursuits. In addition to tools for basic survival they began to make equipment that had aesthetic value: Some of the implements they made show signs of being crafted for beauty as well as utility. At the same time, some people were fashioning things that had no practical use at all. Stone pipes, ornamental beads of bird bones or animal teeth—these and other objects suggest that Archaic Indians had leisure to think about more than their next meal.

This evidence is further reinforced by the greater attention the Archaic people paid to burial of their dead. Although no graves dating from the Archaic period have been found in the Piedmont, they have been uncovered elsewhere in the Southeast. The Indians wrapped the corpses in hides, then placed them in graves, adding containers of red ochre, weapons, tools, and even dogs before covering the body with earth. These activities clearly indicate that the Archaic people had developed a religion and followed rituals prescribed by their system of beliefs. Freeing hands and minds from a constant search for the essentials of daily life had led to a more complex way of life that nourished the spirit as well as the body.

Just as the Paleo-Indian culture gave way to that of the Archaic, so too did the Archaic develop into a new way of life known as the Woodland culture. Archaeologists believe that some aspects of this new way of life originated in the woodland areas that covered all but the extreme south of what is now the eastern United States. Gradually this way of life moved westward across the continent. As with the earlier shift from Paleo-Indian to Archaic cultures, the transition from Archaic to Woodland was gradual, but around 3000 B.P. the way of life began to change. People of the Woodland period owed much to their ancestors, including the knowledge of hunting and gathering, respect for the dead, even pipes and ornaments. But alongside the old came much that was new. The art of making pottery from clay was one important development. Woodland potters became experts in the manufacture of bowls, pipes, and containers of all sizes and shapes. They often decorated their pieces by pressing a paddle wrapped with cord or hides into the clay while it was still wet. Some of these pots were made to hold new foods, for it was during the Woodland period that Indians became farmers as well as hunters and gatherers. The first crops the Indians raised were gourds and squash. Later they added a third, corn, which became as important to a Woodland Indian's diet as mammoth meat had been to the Paleo-Indians.

Just why and how Archaic hunters and gatherers became Woodland potters and farmers is not certain. No major shift in the climate occurred this time as it had earlier to force changes in the Indians' way of life. The best explanation lies to the south, in Mexico and Central America. It was there, among the Maya and other complex societies that were culturally more advanced than the people living in what is now the eastern United States, that agriculture was first developed in America. Corn, gourds, and squash are all tropical plants, and the secrets of growing them probably spread northward from these southern civilizations, eventually reaching what became the eastern United States.

Although it is a mystery as to how pottery and agriculture reached eastern Indians, it is no secret how these

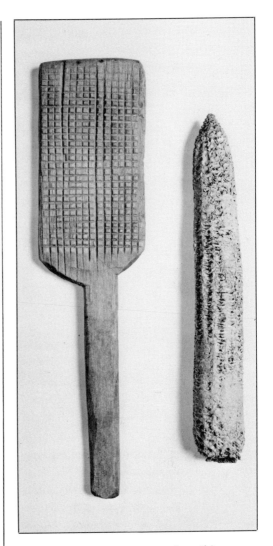

Indians used instruments such as this pottery paddle (left) and corncob to decorate their pottery. When the tool was pressed against a wet piece of pottery, the design would be transferred onto the vessel. The technique of pottery making first appeared in North America during the Woodland period and was introduced to the Piedmont Indians by people from across the Appalachian Mountains.

This mound of earth in northwestern Georgia was at one time the community of Etowah, a leading center of the Mississippian culture. The town's inhabitants were the prehistoric ancestors of the Cherokee Indians.

revolutionary practices reached the Indians of the Piedmont region: They were brought to the area by intruders from the West. During the early Woodland period, for reasons that remain unknown, people from what is now Kentucky crossed the Appalachian Mountains and followed the river courses down into the southern Piedmont. They brought with them the knowledge of pottery making, and clay pots quickly replaced the vessels earlier Indians had carved from soapstone, a soft stone primarily composed of talc and chlorite. These newcomers from the west all spoke different forms of the same language family known as Siouan, so-called because its best known speakers are the Sioux of the Great Plains. These Siouan speakers were the ancestors of the tribes European colonists were to encounter in the southern Piedmont more than a thousand years later, among them the Saponi, Tutelo, Keyauwee, and Catawbas.

About 600 years ago another wave of immigrant Indians, these from the lower Mississippi River valley, entered the southern Piedmont region and settled near what is now Camden, South Carolina, and Mt. Gilead, North Carolina. These invaders, who were part of a sophisticated culture known as Mississippian, were very different from the peoples of the Piedmont. Their appearance was different, they spoke a different language, and they had a more complex culture than the Piedmont tribes did, a culture marked by powerful leaders who ruled over large territories and many peoples. Mississippians built large earth hills or mounds for their temples and expected others to bow down to the glory of their gods. Little is known about these intruders, but it is clear that the Piedmont Indians did not like them. Warfare with the newcomers was probably common, as the Piedmont Indians resisted Mississippian pressure to move deeper into the interior and the Mississippians' desire to rule over them. Over time some Piedmont potters copied the types of pottery made by Mississippian artisans, but in general Mississippian intruders had little more effect than that.

The Piedmont Indians had become used to change long before Hernando de Soto marched through the region in 1540. Although the first Europeans to explore America are said to have connected the Old World and the New, these early explorers in fact connected two worlds, both of them old. Neither would ever be the same again. ▲

Margaret Brown, photographed by Frank G. Speck in 1922.

LIFE AMONG
THE
PIEDMONT PEOPLES

When Hernando de Soto entered the Piedmont in 1540, the name *Catawba* apparently designated a small tribe living along the Catawba River on the border between what are now North and South Carolina. The origin and meaning of the word *Catawba* is a mystery. The Indians of this area actually called themselves *yeh is-WAH h'reh*, meaning "people of the river," or *i-yeh yeh*, which translates simply as "people." Catawba, then, was an imported word pinned on "Esaws" (the colonists' pronunciation of the Catawbas' name) by outsiders, although it is not known by whom. Some scholars think Catawba is a word in the language of the Choctaw tribe of Mississippi and Alabama. Others believe it is a word in the language of the Shawnee or Delaware tribes and applies to anyone living in the Piedmont. One interpretation is that it means "people of the river with broken banks," another, "people of the fork." Scholars, however, remain uncertain as to its true meaning.

Shortly after 1700, *Catawba* became the general term used by the colonists for all of the tribes living in the Catawba River valley. Eventually the definition of the word was expanded to refer not only to the Catawba tribe and its neighbors but also to Indians from farther away who had migrated to the Catawba River valley. Some of these migrants had traveled great distances: A few families of Natchez Indians, for instance, came all the way from Louisiana. Most, however, were the Catawbas' neighbors, and upon joining the Catawbas they discovered that they had much in common with their hosts. From the Santee and Wateree tribes living downriver from the Catawbas, to the Saponi, Cheraw, and Keyauwee tribes that came from North Carolina and Virginia, these Indians were, like Catawbas themselves, residents of the southern Piedmont.

This band of what European colonists called "hilly country" runs all the way from New York to Georgia. Its terrain is marked by rolling hills that are cut by rivers flowing swiftly from the mountains to the sea. Rich soil is found along the banks of the rivers, and the hills are covered with large trees such as oak and hickory. Because the Piedmont Indians spoke similar languages and had learned to survive among the rivers and hills, fields and forests, they came to live in similar ways, similar enough that all of the region's Indians—from Catawbas to Waterees—are commonly called "Piedmont peoples."

Because the Catawba Nation today is descended from all of the Piedmont peoples, it is important to include these other Indians when telling the Catawba story. It is also essential, because the clues needed to understand this story are very difficult to uncover for any one of these Piedmont tribes alone. Historians studying the past commonly rely on written documents to discover what life was like. Learning about Indian history is harder. No Catawbas learned to write until the late 18th century, so we cannot turn to written documents to discover their thoughts in earlier times. Many European colonists could write, and some of them wrote about Indians. Relatively few of them, however, wrote about the Catawbas. Writings that do exist have come from the pens of outsiders unfamiliar with Catawba ways, people who often misunderstood or distorted Indian culture.

By combining the written record with archaeological findings, by ranging widely across the Piedmont to include Indians closely related to and ultimately united with the Catawbas, and finally by filling in the gaps still remaining with evidence from other southeastern Indians, it is possible to paint a picture of life in the Piedmont before the arrival of Europeans changed Indian culture forever.

To the first Europeans who encountered these Indians, it was more like visiting another world than merely visiting another land. Not only was this new land's terrain wild and exotic, but the inhabitants themselves appeared very strange to the early European arrivals. It was not so much the Indians' brown skin, black hair, and piercing dark eyes that they found so unusual, but what the natives did to make themselves handsome. They grew their fingernails very long, and the men fixed their hair in what appeared to the explorers to be very odd ways: Some Indians left a ridge of hair down the center of their head; others had one long clump of hair in back that to the newcomers looked like "a Horse's Tail." The Indians also oiled their hair with bear grease to fix it into assorted shapes. They rubbed more of this grease on their bodies to keep out the cold and ward off insects. On special occasions they painted their skin—especially their faces—with roots that were ground into powder and added to water. When they went to war, for example, Indian men painted their faces red with a black circle around one eye and white around the other. The Indians encountered by the first Europeans wore animal pelts as clothing and often adorned themselves with bracelets and necklaces made of shells, animal teeth, or copper.

Depending on the time of year, Indians of the southern Piedmont could be found in different regions. During the fall and winter they lived in hunting camps scattered across the ridges and hills where deer and other game congregated. From these camps the men went out in search of food. They were now armed with the bow and arrow, a development of the Woodland period that had replaced the atlatl as the hunter's favorite weapon. Sometimes hunters would travel alone, disguising themselves in a deerskin and stealthily creeping up on their prey. At other times they would go out together on fire hunts. This technique involved setting fire to the perimeter of a large circle of land and driving the flames—along with the frightened game—toward the center, where the animals could be slain in large numbers. While the men hunted, the women, children, and old people remained back at the camp, ready to prepare the meat and hides when the hunters returned.

Some of the men who set out from the camp in the fall and winter were hunting other Indians, not deer or bear. Among the Indians of the southern Piedmont, as among all eastern Indians, warfare was part of life. Far from being the "bloodthirsty savages" that they are often portrayed as—barbarians who killed and scalped for no reason— Indians had developed a form of conflict that had its own rules and codes.

HINDE·DE·LORANBEC·

By the time the first Europeans arrived in the Americas, the bow and arrow was the Indians' primary hunting weapon. This illustration appeared in the Histoire naturelle des Indes, *(Natural History of the Indies), one of the earliest records of European exploration in the New World, published in the 1590s.*

Catawbas and other eastern tribes believed that the soul of a person who was killed demanded some kind of satisfaction before it could rest in peace. To ease that soul's pain, the men of the tribe went out in small bands to seek revenge for the death of a fellow mem-

Tree saplings bent and tied together formed the dome-shaped framework of the Catawbas' houses.

ber. Sneaking up on an enemy town or camp, the warriors would usually attack at dawn, killing some townspeople and capturing others. The dead were scalped so that the victorious warriors could bring home proof of their deed to mourning relatives. The captives were either adopted by their captors to replace the deceased or tortured to avenge the loved one's death. This form of warfare, called mourning war, was a means the Indians devised to help the living cope with death. It was also a means of earning respect: The warrior who brought back a scalp or prisoner, like the hunter who returned with a carcass or pelt, won the admiration of his people.

Warfare, like hunting, was generally a cold-weather occupation. In spring and summer, on the other hand, the uplands were empty. As winter drew to a close the Indians of the southern Piedmont moved to the rivers and streams, where the soil was best for growing crops. The Indians had no cattle, horses, or pigs, so their fields did not have to be fenced in for protection against these creatures. Nor did they need fences to divide the fields, for they believed that the land belonged to everyone. All the people planted in the same field, and sections of that field might "belong" only to those who used it. A section that was abandoned became community property again, to be taken up by anyone who needed it.

The European newcomers were surprised to find that the farmers who toiled in the fields were women, not men. Although the men would help clear a new field and the young men do the planting, the rest—hoeing, weeding, harvesting—was women's work. What appeared to the Europeans to be a patchwork of untidy fields was actually a well-planned system of horticulture. Little hills of earth containing corn, beans, and squash were spaced about three or four feet apart. The Indians planted the three crops together in every hill, rather than keeping each in a separate field. This method had several advantages: The hills prevented soil erosion, preserved fertility, made weeding easier, and were well suited for corn, which needs good drainage and secure anchoring for its tall stalks.

Combining corn with other plants also made sense because the cornstalks could serve as bean poles. The beans in turn slowed the soil exhaustion that corn causes. Squash plants, which covered the ground, further helped prevent erosion and discourage weeds.

After passing through the Indians' fields, a visitor would have come upon their houses, usually located in a cluster nearby. Often they were protected by a palisade, or circular wall of upright logs erected to keep enemies out. Inside the palisade were anywhere from 5 to as many as 15 houses. Woodland Indians, unlike their ancestors, often lived in villages of 100 or more people. The dwellings were circular and made of saplings bent to form a frame, which was then covered with tree bark. The first Europeans who slept in the Catawbas' houses thought they were "as hot as Stoves" and just as dark and smoky. Other than the doorway, only a smoke hole in the roof let in light and air. In the center of the house was a circle of

A modern reproduction of the Catawbas' traditional bark house. After the framework of the house was in place, the outer walls were made of strips of bark and the roof was covered with mats made of cattails.

rocks that served as the fireplace, and on the dirt floor were platforms with reed mats that the Indians used as beds.

Every dwelling housed 10 or more people, all of whom were related to one another. Several generations of a family usually lived together. The family, or kinfolk, were very important to the Indians of the southern Piedmont. From the moment a child was born, he or she automatically became part of a large network of relatives who resided in the village. Besides the mother and father, there were aunts, uncles, and other relatives responsible for bringing up the children, teaching them the ways of the tribe, protecting them from harm, and, if harm came, avenging a person's injury or death. Family defined who a Catawba was, decided whom a young person could marry, and determined whom a warrior was responsible for defending.

Important as kinfolk were to the life of a village, the settlement was a community, not a collection of families and houses. Sometimes this community was part of a group of related communities, often called a tribe by Europeans. The people of a tribe, whether living in one or several communities, were held together by a feeling of common identity that was tied to their sense of having a shared past as well as a shared present and future. The Indians perpetuated this feeling of belonging in a variety of ways. The men went out together on war parties or on hunting expeditions. The women worked together in the fields and berry patches.

Marriages helped cement bonds between families in a village, and when disaster struck—a fire, for example—the entire community turned out to help the victims replace food, clothing, and household items.

The layout of the village itself helped keep the community spirit alive. The houses were arrayed along the inside wall of the palisade, which left the center open for communal activities such as dances and contests. Another favorite gathering place was the sweathouse, a small clay hut in or near the village that was similar to a sauna. Most important and prominent was the council house. Not only was this building bigger than a typical house—it could hold everyone in the village—but it was square, not round, and its roof was made of reeds rather than bark. It was here that the Indians welcomed all visitors, and here they met to talk over issues of common concern. All the Indians could attend such discussions, but usually the leaders made the decisions concerning the best plan of action for the tribe. The leaders were generally older men from each family who, having proved themselves as expert hunters, brave warriors, eloquent speakers, or men of wisdom, had earned the respect of the people.

Among these leaders one man stood out as chief, or, in Catawba, *eractasswa*. The colonists thought of this man as a king or emperor, but although he was descended from earlier chiefs as a king would be, he was far from being the kind of powerful monarch with which

Europeans were familiar. Catawbas were too independent to allow anyone to hold such power over them. An eractasswa sat on no throne, wore no crown, and had little real power. He could only persuade people to do something; he could not force them. His main job was to greet and house visitors, speak to the outside world on behalf of his people, and serve as a sort of "master of ceremonies" at public gatherings. Even though he lacked real power, the chief was a busy man, for the Indians had a full schedule of rituals for him to preside over every year. Sometimes they celebrated victories over enemies or a good hunting season; at other times they mourned losses or the death of loved ones. Happy or sad, each occasion meant a night of feasting, dancing, and singing and served as yet another means of keeping a tribe united.

At all these public occasions another man stood at the side of the eractasswa. This man was easily recognized because he wore a cloak made of feathers or cut his hair in an unusual way or hung a sack of roots, bark, or berries around his neck. This was the tribe's religious healer, and the cloak, haircut, and bag were symbols of his status. He served as both a religious leader and a curer. As a young man he had learned the secrets of his craft from an old religious healer who in turn had learned them from his predecessor. Among these secrets was the knowledge of which plants, properly prepared, could cure ailments, from an arrow wound to a stomach-

A ceremonial staff used by Catawba religious healers. Because of their ability to cure ailments and contact the spirit world, religious healers were revered, and often feared, by their fellow tribespeople.

ache. But knowing which berry to pick or which bark to strip, and how to prepare and administer the various healing plants was only part of the religious healer's knowledge. He also depended on his access to the unseen forces and beings, the spirit world, that the Indians of the southern Piedmont believed controlled life and death. Because spirits, or gods, caused illness and injury, only they could prevent or remove them, and it was up to the religious healer to reach the spirit world through prayers and rituals. Although Europeans scoffed at these healers and called their antics "quackship," their cures often worked. "Indian physicians," as they were called by the colonists, successfully healed wounds and cured illnesses that baffled the best doctors the Europeans had.

Europeans were as quick to call Indian religion superstition or devil worship as they were to dismiss Indian religious healers as frauds. The Indians sat in no church, read no Bible, worshiped no single god, and feared no devil; rather, they recognized many good and evil spirits. Their way of worshiping seemed ludicrous, if not blasphemous, to Europeans. However, it has been said that one person's religion is another's superstition, and Indians found Christianity every bit as strange. In fact, though on the surface they appear very different, the two religions are in some ways similar. Both believe people have souls, both believe in life after death, both believe that unseen beings govern the affairs of this world,

and both follow rituals designed to thank, worship, and beseech those unseen beings.

The first Europeans who came upon the Piedmont peoples noticed not only their way of life but also their personal characteristics. They found the Indians to be very hospitable, generously providing food and shelter to anyone who visited them. The Indians were very polite as well, both to each other and to strangers. It was considered bad manners to speak harshly to family or neighbors, and Europeans, who were generally quick to show anger, were amazed at how peaceful life in an Indian village was. Indians, however, were not the serious, almost stone-faced people that they are often portrayed as being. They laughed often and loudly—especially at Europeans, who did not know the local language and customs and, like any ignorant tourists, frequently made fools of themselves. Indians also knew how to have fun. In addition to dancing and singing, they loved to gamble, and they bet on almost everything. Ball games somewhat like modern lacrosse were popular, as were contests played with reeds or stones that colonists called "Indian cards" and "Indian dice."

It was much easier to share a meal or a laugh with these people than it was to get them to talk about themselves or to reach a decision. Though polite and generous, Indians were wary of outsiders. Moreover, because no one person had the power to make a decision, it could take a long time for the mem-

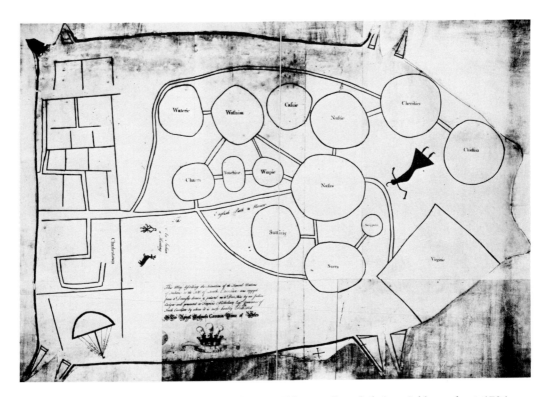

A map showing the location of the Catawbas, or "Nassaw," and their neighbors about 1724. The map was drawn on a deerskin by an Indian chief and dedicated to the Prince of Wales, later King George II.

bers of a tribe to talk things over and make up their collective mind as to what to do. Archaeologists have concluded that Piedmont Indians were conservative because they were slow to adopt new fashions in pottery or arrowheads, and this seems to fit what we know from other sources. The Catawbas of the Woodland period had found a fertile home and achieved a comfortable balance—between hunting and farming, between winter and summer—that they saw no reason to upset by changing their ways and embracing new things.

Soon after the first Europeans arrived, however, the balance the Catawbas had struck was turned upside down. As before, the Catawbas would survive this latest upheaval in their way of life, but their world would be drastically different. ▲

Catawba children, photographed by Frank G. Speck in 1922.

MICROBES
AND
MUSKETS

Although by 1540 the Catawbas were accustomed to change, the changes Europeans would cause in their lives were far greater and occurred much faster than anything the Indians had known before. The rapidity and extent of these changes was not caused by hordes of European colonists suddenly taking over the Catawbas' land: Not until the 18th century did settlers begin to move into the Piedmont. Long before then, however, European settlements along the Atlantic coast were influencing Catawba history through microbes, microorganisms that cause disease, and muskets, those very visible symbols of the new goods Europeans introduced to America.

Europeans quite literally made American Indians sick. When Hernando de Soto marched through the region in 1540 he saw many empty villages. The inhabitants had died from diseases that had been brought inland from Spanish outposts on the coast. The arrival of the English several decades later had the same deadly effect: The diseases they brought killed Indians by the thousands. In 1709 an English colonist estimated that over the previous 50 years only 1 Carolina Indian in 7 had survived; the rest had died of disease.

At the time, most colonists believed that the death of the Indians was part of God's plan to make the European conquest of America easier by destroying the native population. It is now known that Indians died in such large numbers because they had had no previous exposure to the viruses and bacteria that cause smallpox, measles, yellow fever, and many other communicable diseases. Unlike populations in Asia, Africa, and Europe that had long been exposed to such diseases, the peoples of the Americas had acquired no immunity to these invisible invad-

This 1726 map of Carolina reveals the colonists' increased awareness of Indian populations to the west of English settlements along the coast.

ers. An outbreak of smallpox or measles among Europeans was a serious matter, and many people died. An outbreak of the same disease among the Catawbas was a catastrophe. Sometimes almost everyone died. In 1759, for example, when smallpox swept through the Catawba Nation for the fourth time in a century, two of every three Indians perished in less than three months. From the tens of thousands of Indians living in the Piedmont before European contact, the population had fallen to less than 1,000 by 1760. Throughout North America it was the newcomers' diseases, more than their armies, that conquered the natives.

It is difficult to imagine what life must have been like for those few Indians who survived an outbreak of measles or smallpox. The web of relatives among which each person lived was torn to pieces as aunts and cousins, brothers and mothers perished. Gone, too, were huge chunks of the past. Sickness hit the elderly especially hard, and the old people were the ones who knew the stories and songs, the skills and secrets passed down from earlier times. In addition the authority of the religious healers was undermined, as their potions and prayers had no effect against these devastating epidemics. In some cases there were simply too few people left to carry on their daily life as they had. When a small tribe's numbers were reduced from several hundred to fewer than 100, they could no longer defend themselves against their enemies, find eligible marriage partners, clear fields, hold tribal ceremonies, or hunt communally.

Somehow the Catawbas and other Piedmont Indians managed to overcome these difficulties. Many moved in with nearby tribes that also needed more people in order to carry on. These tribal mergers were not uncommon. In 1701, for example, the people of the Eno and Shakori tribes, who lived along the Neuse River, united in one town. Soon afterward the Saponi, Tutelo, and Keyauwee did the same. As disease struck again and again, these tribes and others headed for the Catawba River valley, where they joined with the Catawbas to become part of the Catawba Nation. Thus sickness brought the far-flung Piedmont Indians, now much reduced in numbers, together in one place.

Once these peoples had settled into new homes, they began putting their life back in order. They rebuilt the web of kinfolk so that they again lived with an assortment of relatives. The Indians also continued to respect the old people of the tribe. "Old Age [is] held in as great Veneration amongst these Heathens," wrote John Lawson, a colonist who visited the Catawbas in 1701, "as amongst any People you shall meet withal in any Part of the World." In council it was the elders who spoke first, and at public festivals it was they who sang of old times. Clearly the loss of so many old people had made those who survived even more valuable because they were so rare.

Although religious healers had failed to cure the new sicknesses, they, like the elderly, still continued to have influence over the tribe. In part their authority survived because their other powers—attending to wounds, treating common illnesses, and so on—were undiminished. They also remained important because they learned to change with the changing times. One religious healer of the Santee tribe was especially clever. Around 1700 he fell ill with a disease that had the effect of destroying the sufferer's nose. He fled to the woods with a companion who was similarly afflicted. They managed to save their lives, but when they returned the tribe was amazed to see them without noses and, as John Lawson reported, "enquir'd of them where they had been all that Time, and what were become of their Noses?"

The religious healer's prestige was at stake here, for his failure to cure him-

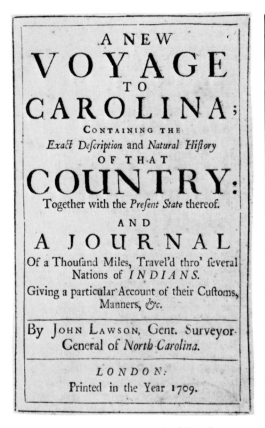

A NEW
VOYAGE
TO
CAROLINA;
CONTAINING THE
Exact Description and *Natural History*
OF THAT
COUNTRY:
Together with the *Present State* thereof.
AND
A JOURNAL
Of a Thousand Miles, Travel'd thro' several
Nations of *INDIANS.*
Giving a particular Account of their Customs,
Manners, *&c.*

By JOHN LAWSON, Gent. Surveyor-
General of *North-Carolina.*

LONDON:
Printed in the Year 1709.

In 1701, as surveyor-general of North Carolina, the English colonist John Lawson visited the Catawbas. Eight years later he published A New Voyage to Carolina, *which included valuable descriptions of traditional Catawba life before it was drastically changed by European culture.*

self made it look as if he had lost his power to communicate with the gods who sent sickness or dispensed cures. However, he managed to wriggle out of this tight spot. "They made Answer, That they had been conversing with the white Man above, (meaning God Almighty). . . ," Lawson wrote, "he

being much pleas'd with their Ways, . . . had promis'd to make their Capacities equal with the white People in making Guns, Ammunition, etc., in Retalliation [exchange] of which, they had given him their Noses." The quick-thinking healer, like the Piedmont Indians after terrible epidemics struck, managed to survive the disaster and find some way out of the chaos that disease had caused. For him it meant the loss of a nose; for others it meant the loss of kin, of tribal identity, or of homeland as they uprooted themselves to join with others in similar predicaments.

That the religious healer saved himself by mentioning "Guns, Ammunition, etc." indicates how vital these weapons had already become to the Catawbas and their neighbors. "They think themselves undrest and not fit to walk abroad unless they have their gun on their shoulder and their shot-bag by their side," wrote one Virginian in the late 17th century, and he did not exaggerate. Next to disease, trade goods supplied by the colonists had the greatest impact on Catawba society.

Setting up this trade was easy. Both the Indians and the English were experienced traders. Tribes had been trading among themselves for centuries, and the English came to America in part to expand their country's trade. Each possessed goods that the other wanted. For the most part Catawbas traded deerskins, which were shipped to England to be made into leather for breeches, gloves, and various other items. They also traded war captives from enemy tribes, who were in demand as slaves to work on the plantations of colonial farmers. In return, the Indians received a wide range of wares, from muskets and knives to kettles and scissors, from cloth and beads to rum and paint. After 1650, when traders from the colony of Virginia began visiting the southern Piedmont, the volume of goods traded grew rapidly. Many a Virginian, such as the prominent landholder and successful trader William Byrd, made a fortune from the skins and slaves he carried back from the Piedmont. After Charleston was founded in 1670, Carolina traders also began visiting the Piedmont with a long line of packhorses in tow. These caravans, sometimes numbering up to 100 horses, were loaded down with an assortment of merchandise that would be traded for skins or slaves.

Because the colonists were so eager to get the Indians' goods, the Catawbas at first were able to set the rules of the trading game, and colonists who hoped to make a profit had to go along with these rules. Wise traders who arrived at a Catawba village learned the proper etiquette, greeting the leaders politely in the Indians' language, not in English. If they expected to stay for a while they would also be smart to marry a woman of the village, a union Indians considered an important sign of friendship. Some colonists fled when invited to their own wedding to an Indian woman: One sneaked out of town after dark to escape the Indian matchmakers.

A deerskin dries on a hide-stretching frame. The Catawbas traded their bountiful supply of deerskins to colonial traders from Virginia and Carolina in exchange for a wide assortment of European goods.

Most, however, realized that these "Indian wives" were good for business. They helped the trader learn the language, cooked and cleaned for him, and introduced him to potential customers.

It was probably more difficult for these traders to get used to Indian ways of measuring products than to Indian ways of marriage. To Catawbas a necklace of beads was not a foot or a yard long but an arm's length, and they cared not at all that some people's arms were longer than others. Similarly Indians bought rum not in pints, quarts, or gallons but by the mouthful. The customer would take a swig from the trader's bottle and then spit it into a bowl so that he or she could drink it later. Although this was as strange to the colonists as it seems to us today, the traders said nothing, for this was the Indian way.

Just as Catawbas expected colonial traders to follow the Indian manner of doing things, they also expected the

William Byrd, a successful trader and planter, was the first of several generations of Byrds to trade with the Catawbas.

traders' goods to fit old uses and established tastes. Indians were conservative: They bought goods that suited their traditional ways rather than changing their ways to suit the new goods. Most of the merchandise Catawbas bought simply did the same job as their traditional equipment, only better. Thus a brass kettle was sturdier than a clay pot; an iron hoe, ax, or knife had a sharper blade than one made of stone; garments and blankets made of woven cloth were more comfortable and more durable than those made of skins or furs; and a musket ball was better for killing than an arrow. Other trade goods were not better, just substitutes for what natives had always used: Glass beads replaced seashell necklaces and bracelets, and Indian dancers now attached metal horse bells to their ankles instead of rattles made from a turtle's shell. Other new products were used to make the Indians' old tools: Broken glass, for example, could be turned into arrowheads.

Of all the trade goods Indians obtained, only liquor proved severely disruptive. For reasons that are still unclear, American Indians in general are particularly affected by alcoholic beverages, which were introduced by Europeans. The Catawbas were no exception. It was, the Indians said soon after first tasting it, a "poisonous plant" that made people sick. Yet they could not resist it. Hunters might sell all of their deerskins for liquor and then drink away a whole season's profits in one day. Some Indians under the influ-

This trading station in Petersburg, Virginia, built by Peter Jones around 1675, was the northern terminus of the trade route leading to the Catawbas' villages in Carolina. The photograph was made in 1865 by Civil War photographer Mathew Brady.

ence of liquor fell into fires and burned themselves, others attacked relatives and townsfolk. No one, not even the Catawbas' religious healers, could find an antidote to this poison.

Despite the problems caused by their fondness for rum, until around 1700, Catawbas controlled the way trade with colonists was carried out.

The Indians were in charge because the colonists' goods were not yet essential to them. If the color was wrong or the trader impolite, they could always go back to the clay pots, the deerskin clothing, the bow and arrow. Soon after 1700, however, this changed. It was not that the Catawbas suddenly forgot how to chip arrowheads or shape clay pots.

But Indians who were carrying muskets and cooking in brass kettles had less need to practice their old craft skills. As their skills diminished, it became more difficult for them to manufacture good tools and, therefore, more difficult to get along without the substitutes traders brought. What had once been luxuries had now become necessities, and without realizing what was happening, Catawbas were becoming dependent on products that they could not make for themselves.

The average colonial trader realized this before the Catawbas did. After 1700 this knowledge gave him the courage to begin doing things his way. From being polite guests, many traders—particularly those from Charleston—now became cheats and thieves. They diluted their rum with water, raised their prices, forced Indians to carry heavy packs, stole food, and beat anyone who dared to complain. Even worse, when an Indian fell too deeply in debt, more than one trader enslaved the customer who owed him money and sold him to planters in Charleston to pay off the loan. Catawbas were not alone in suffering these abuses. Along the coast south of Charleston, where heavy trading took place with the Yamasee Indians, the traders' abuses were even worse. Finally, after years of mistreatment, the Indians rebelled. In the spring of 1715 the Yamasee, Catawbas, and almost every other Indian tribe that traded with the English in Carolina launched an all-out attack on the colony. The Yamasee War, during which

A Catawba warrior, sketched in 1771 by an unknown artist. The Catawbas had reputations as fierce and fearless warriors, and their fighting skills were recognized by Indians and non-Indians alike.

hundreds of colonists and Indians died, had begun.

If the Catawbas had not realized their dependence on the English before then, they knew it within a few months of declaring war. At first the Indians won a series of battles. By June, Catawba warriors, having destroyed several frontier forts, were only 15 or 20 miles from the provincial capital at Charleston. They got no closer, however. In that month a surprise attack by an army of colonists, African slaves, and coastal Indians killed 60 Catawbas. The rest were unable to carry on the fight because they ran out of ammunition. Without fresh supplies from the traders the Indians had nothing left with which to fight. By the end of the summer of 1715 the Catawbas and their allies were asking for peace. They now knew, as one dejected chief put it, that "we cannot live without the assistance of the English."

By the time the final peace treaty ending the war was signed in April 1717, the Catawbas had been in contact with Europeans for almost two centuries. It had not been a happy chapter in Catawba history. Disease had killed many, and most of the rest, once scattered across the Piedmont as separate tribes, were now huddled together in six villages along the Catawba River. Trade had placed in Catawba hands many new and wonderful things. But the Indians' joy in these prizes soon turned to sorrow as they realized that owning them had a hidden cost. It left them dependent on the alien intruders, and it did not look like the "white Man above" would teach them how to make their own guns after all.

Still, despite all the tragedies and the setbacks, the Catawbas' spirit was not broken. Their faith in their own way remained strong, even after losing battles to European diseases and colonial armies. When, at the 1717 peace negotiations that ended the Yamasee War, colonists invited Catawba leaders to learn English and convert to Christianity, the Indians flatly refused. As one colonist reported, they "asked leave to be excused from becoming as we are, for they thought it hard, that we should desire them to change their manners and customs, since they did not desire us to turn Indians." Although Catawbas now admitted that they needed the English, they were not about to become like the English themselves. ▲

Doris Wheelock, photographed by Frank G. Speck in 1922.

WARRIORS
AND
DIPLOMATS

If it was difficult for the Catawba people to admit that they could not live without the English, it was even more difficult for them to learn how to live *with* them. The problem was that the Catawbas and colonists neither understood nor liked each other very much, and the bitter battles of the Yamasee War of 1715 only deepened their hatred. According to James Adair, an 18th-century South Carolinian who frequently traded with the Catawbas, the Indians had "an inexpressible contempt of the white people." They called whites "the accursed people." Colonists felt the same way about Indians. One South Carolina official wrote that Indians "are a savage, cruel, perfidious, revengefull sett of Men."

To add to the problem of mutual dislike, Catawbas found that their own value as business partners was declining. Soon after the Yamasee War ended, colonists again began flocking to the Catawbas' villages and flooding them with trade goods. By 1740, however, eager Catawba hunters had depleted the deer population in the Piedmont, leaving the Indians fewer and fewer deerskins to swap for the traders' wares. As defeated enemies who no longer made a profit for colonial merchants, the Catawbas had little that would make colonists want to befriend them.

Yet the Catawba Nation still had one thing the colonists needed: its ability to protect South Carolina. The danger to the colony came from several directions. First, the French, enemies of the British, occupied Canada to the north and the Louisiana Territory to the south and west and were friendly with many of the Indian nations located between those two regions. Thus South Carolina, like all of England's American colonies, fretted constantly about bands of French soldiers or Indian warriors—or both—invading the colony. The Catawba settlements along the Catawba River blocked one of the main highways an invader might choose. Just by being there, then, the Nation was, as one strategist in Charleston put it, "an excellent Barrier to this Province."

Second, the colonists faced another enemy closer to home: Afro-American slaves. The trade in Indian war captives, a trade in which Catawbas participated, was never sufficient to meet the needs of colonial planters. The owners of large plantations relied on enslaved laborers brought from Africa by European traders to work in their tobacco and rice fields and households. By 1708 the population of South Carolina was 50 percent black, and from that year on the white colonists were outnumbered by their Afro-American slaves.

In September 1739 a group of African slaves rose up, killed many whites, and almost escaped from South Carolina before they were stopped by colonial militia. Realizing now just how vulnerable they were, colonists were glad to have the Catawbas nearby, ready to help put down any slave unrest. "It is necessary," one prominent South Carolinian wrote in 1754, "to keep up that [Catawba] nation . . . to be a Check upon the runaway Slaves who might otherwise get to a head [escape] in the Woods."

Last but not least of the dangers facing the colonists of South Carolina came from the Catawbas themselves. True, these Indians had been defeated in the Yamasee War, but they were by no means conquered. Colonists were afraid that if they angered the Catawbas again, the Nation's 700 warriors would mount another attack. A war with these Indians was much to be feared for a variety of reasons. First, the Catawbas' location, which made them so valuable for keeping French soldiers out of the colony and runaway slaves in, also made them especially perilous as enemies. One frightened colonist observed that if Catawbas ever decided on war "the[y] would be worse than twice the Number of other Indians[,] the[y] being so well a[c]quainted with the Country."

An announcement of the sale of slaves in Charleston. By the early 1700s there were more blacks than whites in South Carolina.

Second, Catawbas had a reputation as being the best fighters in the East. James Glen, governor of South Carolina from 1743 to 1755, believed that Catawbas were "the bravest Fellows on the Continent of America." One of Glen's fellow South Carolinians agreed that "in War, they are inferior [to] no Indians whatever."

By 1750 the Catawbas claimed as enemies no fewer than 11 different Indian peoples. Of these their greatest foes were the Six Nations of Iroquois Indians, who lived primarily in New York. The Catawbas and Iroquois were old and bitter enemies. Iroquois war parties bound for Catawba villages would head south on the "Warriors' Path," which ran along the foothills of the Appalachian Mountains. Once there, the warriors hid in the woods, ambushing an isolated hunting camp or cornfield, killing a few people and capturing others to carry home. Catawbas often pursued these retreating war parties as far as Virginia or even Pennsylvania, determined to take revenge for the death of a loved one or to rescue another taken prisoner. Year after year the war raged on and the hatred grew. Colonists observing this rivalry from a safe distance were terrified that Catawbas might turn this energy and skill against them.

No colonist better knew these basic truths about the Catawbas' worth or tried harder to keep them happy than South Carolina governor James Glen. When Glen arrived from London to serve as governor, he tried to learn

James Glen, governor of South Carolina from 1743 to 1755. He made great efforts to establish a good relationship between the Catawbas and the colonists.

everything he could about these people. "The Affairs of this Country are so closely connected and interwoven with Indian Concerns that it is impossible to separate them," he said. "I have taken [a] good deal of pains to arrive at some knowledge in these matters, and I hope I may be allowed to say that I am pretty well acquainted with them." The Catawbas became a special project of his. "Many Nations of Indians think we distinguish you too much," he wrote to his "Good Friends and Loving

Brothers" the Catawbas in 1754, "and that we are more sollicitous of your Welfare than of theirs, . . . and even some white People say, that we make no Difference betwixt you and them." Glen was proud of his colony's record of friendship and "hope[d] it will last while the Sun gives Light."

Despite some distrust and occasional conflicts, Catawbas and colonists maintained favorable relations through diplomacy. Their official relationship often took place at a distance, by letter. Catawbas had no knowledge of writing until Europeans arrived, but they quickly learned the magic contained in marks on paper. By 1701 the Indians were copying English writing, even though they could not read the words they copied. During Glen's administration, he and other officials kept up a lively correspondence with the Catawba Nation. The governor would send a letter "To the brave King Haglar and the Warriors of the Catawba Nation" to ask a favor, complain about Catawba misbehavior, or simply send his regards. A colonial trader would translate the letter into Catawba. The Indian leaders would then have the trader write a response, at the bottom of which the Catawbas would place their marks or "signatures."

Sometimes a letter was not enough, and the two sides met face to face, usually in Charleston. The Catawba delegation could be as small as a half-dozen leaders. Some diplomatic parties, however, numbered more than 50 people and included headmen, young warriors, women, and even children. The colonists worked hard to entertain and impress their visitors. In 1745, for example, Governor Glen received with much ceremony a party of Catawbas and Cherokees. Several troops of cavalry met the Indian ambassadors on the outskirts of town and escorted them to the capital along a route lined by two columns of soldiers. Colonial officials greeted the delegation at the city limits and invited the chiefs to ride through town in the governor's horse-drawn coach. The rest of the Indians followed, marching down Charleston's main streets to the accompaniment of beating drums, flying flags, and cannons booming a salute.

When the Indians arrived at the meeting place of the Provincial Council, the upper branch of the two-house South Carolina legislature, the formal proceedings began. First there was the ceremony of shaking hands, or, more accurately, "shaking arms," which the Catawbas considered essential to getting the discussion off to a good start. The Indians would go around the room grasping each Crown official by the upper arm, until everyone had met each other. After this formality the speeches could begin. These talks were always in the Catawba language. Until 1750 a trader usually interpreted to and from English, but after that the Catawbas had their own interpreter to translate for them. The first Catawba to fill this position was Hixayoura, or "Ears," whose descendants today spell their name Ayers.

Mount Pleasant 25th August 1759

Beloved Brother

Our Beloved Man Samuel Wyly informs us that you received Our Talk which we sent by your Warriour Capt Adamson, and in answer thereto he informs us, that you will always be ready to give us of Our People all the Marks of kindness in your Power, and that Mr Atkin is the Man who must determine Concerning the Building of a Fort.

We are resolved to remain fast friends to our Father the great King George, and to fight for him & his Beloved People whilst a Man of us is left. but would have our Beloved Brother to consider the dangerousness of our situation, and Order a Fort to be built for us without delay as we have no place of safety for Our wives & Children should we be called out to War, and we fear it may be too long to wait the coming of Mr Atkin, who has promised to come to Our Nation almost two Years ago

We are in Great Want of Ammunition not having a sufficient quantity for our Hunts & much more so if we should be attacked by any of your Enemies, therefore beg your Order us some to be Delivered at Pinetree Store

Sixty Odd of our Warriors are gone along with our Brothers the Virginians to War, under the Command of Capt Airs, Capt John & Capt Strongman

George his mark

Terraykuck his mark

Bully his mark

Prince his mark

John Scott his mark

William Crook his mark

Captain his mark

Lewis John his mark

George his mark

King Hagler his mark

Jemmie his mark

Watura his mark

Hixorenah mark

Hixerleigh mark

Nabree mark

Pake Catt his mark

Top Top his mark Hoy

Robert his mark

Haver his mark

Captain Wood his mark

Chip his mark Peter

Captain Thomas his mark

Captain Whiting his mark

Because the Catawbas themselves could not write, they depended on traders to carry on a substantial correspondence with colonial officials. The Catawba leaders would make a mark beside their names, each of which was attested to by the scribe. Among the signatures on this 1759 letter is that of "King" Hagler, the chief of the Catawba Nation at the time.

To the colonists the Indians' speech, once translated into English, often sounded odd because a Catawba speaker used a set of images to convey his meaning. In talking of friendship, for example, a person might say that Catawbas and colonists were born from one womb, ate from one spoon, smoked from one pipe, and slept by one fire. If all was well, the "path" between the Catawba town and the colonial capital was said to be clean or clear. If trouble arose, however, the Catawba spokesman warned that the path had become bloody or covered with tree stumps. Whether the path at the moment was clear or bloody, after each side had had its say the meeting ended with an exchange of gifts, which to Indians were symbols of friendship. Catawba leaders would present the governor with some deerskins or clay pipes; in return, the governor might give them each a fancy suit of clothes, a silver armband, or a medal. Colonists did not always understand what was going on, with the handshakes, the talk of paths and spoons, and the gifts, but they went along with the ritual to keep their Indian guests happy.

Diplomacy is an art, and during the 1740s and 1750s the Catawbas were lucky to have two eractasswas (chiefs) who excelled at it. The first, Yanabe Ya-

A view of Charles Town (later renamed Charleston), South Carolina, around 1739.

tengway, or Young Warrior, was chief of the Catawba Nation from 1740 to 1749. Governor Glen, who knew Young Warrior well, was convinced that he was "in every respect the greatest man that ever their Nation had produced." Among Catawbas the words of this chief carried great weight, and he used his way with words to become closer friends with the officials of South Carolina. When he died on his way home from a meeting with Glen—killed either by disease or by an enemy raid—the governor was very upset. "As he was a very great Warriour, and a remarkable friend to the English," Glen mourned, "his loss is irreparable."

The next chief, Nopkehe, or Hagler (chief from 1750 to 1763), restored Glen's hope for the Nation's future. Great as Young Warrior was, his successor may have been greater still. Certainly he is the most famous Catawba chief, among both Indians and non-Indians. The citizens of Camden, South Carolina, remember him today as their "patron saint" for his friendliness and helpfulness to the town's founders. Hagler's popularity is easy to understand. He remained a firm friend to the English, yet was committed to his people. He was determined to remain on the Catawbas' ancestral lands and to follow the old ways. At the same time, he knew that the English were now many, the Catawbas few, and it was essential to get along. He was an eloquent speaker and able politician, and flattery was his favorite tool. "Our Brothers the White men of this Province [South Carolina] has always been very good to us," he would say. "I always advise my Men to be kind and obliging to the White People, as they are Brothers[,] and I shall continue to do so and remain their Brother 'till a sharp thing pierces my Breast so that I die."

If Hagler knew how to flatter his allies, he also knew how to scare them. In 1755 an agent of the colony reported that Hagler "with much Assurance demanded of me if the Governor had sent them any Powder and Ball. I told him I knew of none. He said the White

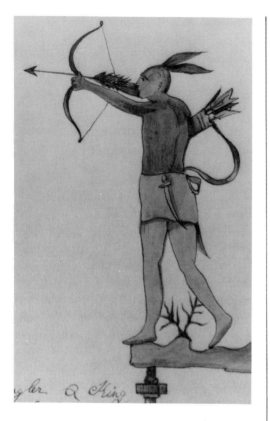

This weathervane in the likeness of Hagler, chief of the Catawba Nation from 1750 to 1763, is on the Town Hall in Camden, South Carolina.

People spoke much and performed but little. . . . " If the colony did not cooperate, the chief said on another occasion, the Nation's "yo[u]ng people who are Already greatly incenced [against South Carolina] perhaps May Not be prevaled Upon from Doing some great Mischief."

If the officials of South Carolina still did not listen to such threats, Hagler had another effective strategy: He could make other friends. The colonies of Vir-

ginia and North Carolina were also eager to have Indian allies, and Hagler worked to "Brighten, and Strengthen, the Chain of Friendship" between the Catawbas and all three colonies. He traveled extensively through the southern colonies to meet with officials on behalf of his Nation. It was on his way back from such a mission in August 1763 that he met his death at the hands of a Shawnee war party.

The leadership of such skilled diplomats as Hagler and Young Warrior benefited the Catawbas in numerous ways. First and foremost was peace with the English, who were now clearly the rulers of the region. Peace was by no means a sure thing; indeed, many people predicted that another conflict like the Yamasee War of 1715 could break out at any time. By carving out diplomatic channels, Young Warrior and Hagler made it more likely that Indians and colonists would talk, not fight, when misunderstandings occurred.

Second, by befriending colonists the Catawbas strengthened their Nation. Because the British were eager to have a sturdy barrier on their frontier, they helped the Catawbas recruit new members. Disease had already caused many decimated tribes to merge with the Catawbas, and officials in South Carolina encouraged this trend. As a result of these tribal mergers, the Catawba Nation became a melting pot of peoples. In the early 1740s a colonist heard more than 20 different languages being spoken by the residents of the Nation's 6 villages. Like immigrants to America, these new members of the Catawba Nation found that through the years old loyalties to one's tribe or group of origin were replaced by new attachments to the "Nation." Cheraws, Waterees, and the other migrants gradually lost their own identity and came to think of themselves as Catawbas. Over time the Nation spoke to the world with a single voice. With the addition of these new-

comers, during the 1750s the Catawba Nation continued to have 500 warriors and about 2,500 people, despite devastating epidemics in 1718 and 1738 that had killed many of its members.

To further bolster the Catawbas' strength, authorities of the British Crown supplied the Nation with large amounts of goods. For the Catawbas, whose deerskin trade was now in decline and who, consequently, no longer

A speech made by Hagler, chief of the Catawbas, on August 29, 1754, translated into English and written down for the governor by the colonist Matthew Toole.

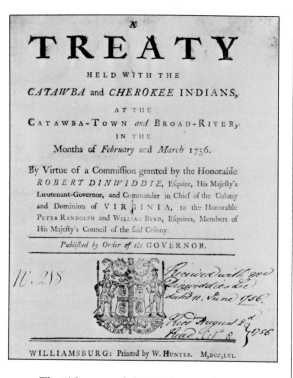

The title page of the 1756 treaty between the Catawbas, the Cherokee, and the colony of Virginia in which the Indians agreed to send warriors to aid the British in the Seven Years' War against France.

William Byrd III, one of the third generation of Byrds to carry on trade with the Catawbas, helped negotiate the 1756 treaty between the colony of Virginia and the Catawba and Cherokee Indians.

received as many goods through trade, this merchandise was essential. A wide variety of "presents" poured through diplomatic channels. Hagler received many gifts in his position as chief, among them a log house, a British flag, a medal, a rifle, and a horse, but he acquired even more for his people. One shipment delivered to the Indians in 1752, for example, included yards of cloth, dozens of shirts, 5 brass kettles, 18 smaller pots, 250 needles, and ½ pound of thread. The same shipment also contained 12 guns, 300 pounds of bullets, 3 dozen knives and the same number of bells, 18 combs, 6 mirrors, 18 pairs of earrings, and more than 400 buttons. Catawba diplomacy had yielded a rich harvest of goods.

In return for their gifts the British colonists obtained loyal friends and staunch allies with considerable talent as warriors. When the Cherokee went to war against South Carolina in 1760, 40 Catawba warriors led by Hagler joined the colonial army marching against the Cherokees' mountain homes. When in 1765 slaves left their plantations and hid out in swamps near Charleston, a Catawba war party came down and, according to one South Carolina official, "partly by the Terror of their Name . . .,apprehended several, and most of the rest of them [the runaways] chose to surrender themselves to their Masters and return to their duty rather than Expose themselves to the Attack of an Enemy so dreaded and so difficult to be . . . evaded."

Most important of all during these years was the Catawbas' service in the Seven Years' War (also called the French and Indian War). In America this conflict, part of a war between France and Great Britain, lasted from 1754 to 1760. (A formal peace was not signed until 1763.) Throughout these years Catawba warriors were much sought after by British commanders. Among those eager to recruit Catawba men was young George Washington, then a colonel in the Virginia militia. Washington knew that Indians' skills as hunters, trackers, and fighters were incomparable. Because many Indians were allies of the French, Washington astutely observed that "unless we have Indians to oppose Indians, we may expect but small success." The young officer's Virginia superiors felt the same way. In February 1756 the colony sent William Byrd III, a grandson of the Virginia trader of the same name, to the Catawba Nation to recruit warriors. Within a month 40 Catawba warriors were on their way to the western fron-

tier of Virginia and Pennsylvania, where most of the fighting took place. Over the next several years other war parties also joined the cause.

Thus diplomacy brought rewards to both sides. In Catawbas, colonists had allies whose reputation as warriors was known from Iroquois villages to Canadian towns to slave quarters. In colonists, Catawbas had suppliers of what Hagler called "the Necessaries of Life." With colonial help, the last of the Piedmont peoples could survive.

This is not to say their way of life was the same, for much had changed even in Hagler's own lifetime. First and most obvious was the fact that by 1750 the Piedmont was almost empty of Indians. Often only the ruins of former Indian sites, such as those places the colonists called "Indian old town" and "Indian old field," served as reminders of the tribes and villages that once had covered the region. It was only along one stretch of the Catawba River, where the Nation's six villages were clustered, that large numbers of Indians could be found. Even these villages, however, did not look the same as they had a generation or two before. The architectural tastes of English colonists were beginning to influence native construction so that some Indian forts and houses were now square instead of round.

The inhabitants of these buildings also looked different than earlier Indians. The mark of the English was everywhere. Some Indians—with names like Brown, Cantey, Bullen, and Evans—were the children of colonial traders

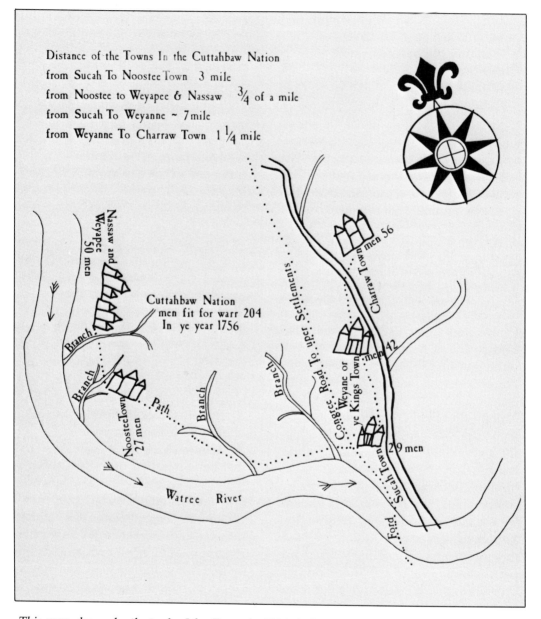

Distance of the Towns In the Cuttahbaw Nation
from Sucah To Noostee Town   3 mile
from Noostee to Weyapee & Nassaw   ¾ of a mile
from Sucah To Weyanne ~ 7 mile
from Weyanne To Charraw Town 1 ¼ mile

Nassaw and Weyapee 50 men

Cuttahbaw Nation men fit for warr 204 In ye year 1756

Charraw Town men 56

Road To uper Settlements

Noostee Town 27 men

Branch

Branch

Path

Branch

Branch

Congree Road To uper Settlements

Weyane or ye Kings Town men 42

Sucah Town 29 men

Ford

Watree   River

This map, drawn by the trader John Evans in 1756, indicates the number and location of Catawba warriors available to assist the British in the Seven Years' War against France. Evans was sent by the governor of South Carolina to determine what aid the Catawba Nation could provide.

and Catawba women and had a foot in both worlds. They and others now preferred cloth garments to skins or furs, and on special occasions some of the important men dressed in the fancy English outfits given to them by officials in Charleston: On their feet were buckled shoes, not moccasins, and they wore blue ruffled shirts and maroon jackets topped off with wigs and hats trimmed with ribbons. On special occasions, too, it was not uncommon to see the Union Jack, the British flag, flying above the chief's house as a symbol of his loyalty to the British Crown.

Catawbas were now riding horses, another custom that had been recently adopted from the English. At first the Indians were awkward riders. According to a Virginia colonist, one chief of the Saponi tribe, after being thrown from a horse several times, "could not imagine what good they were for, if it was not to cripple the Indians." By Hagler's day Catawbas were expert horsemen, and no Indians went anywhere on foot if they could help it. Moreover, some Catawbas were beginning to learn a little English, and almost all of them now followed Hagler and Young Warrior in answering to an English name. In both large ways and small, prolonged contact with another culture was altering the Catawbas' way of life.

Catawbas might speak halting English, ride a horse, wear a wig, and salute the British flag, but they felt no less Catawba. Though much had changed, much remained the same. A Catawba warrior was still feared far and wide, still cut his hair a certain way, and still tattooed his face to show his status. He still prepared for battle with a war dance that recounted his past exploits. Even with a British flag flying over them, chief and council continued to meet to discuss important issues. And the basic rhythms of Catawba life—hunting in fall and winter, planting in spring and summer—remained the same despite fewer deer and a severe drought that plagued the Piedmont through the 1750s.

When William Richardson, a Presbyterian minister, visited the Nation in 1758 to spread the beliefs of Christianity, he got nowhere. Hagler was at least diplomatic, explaining to the clergyman that most of the Indians were away hunting so he could not say whether they would welcome the chance to hear a sermon. Other Catawbas were less polite to the "Sunday Man," as they called all missionaries. In his diary, Richardson wrote that one Catawba warrior informed him that " 'old Indian make no Sabbath and young Indian make no Sabbath' . . . and he was averse to talk to the Rev. so off he went." In 1760 another Catawba, Airs (probably Hixayoura or "Ears"), stated clearly the Catawbas' enduring pride in their own customs. "We Indians are of a different colour from the White people," he told the people of South Carolina, "but the Great Man above has no respect for the white more than the Red." ▲

Joe Saunders, photographed by Frank G. Speck.

POTTERS
AND
PATRIOTS

For about a century after their first contact with the English, and despite frequent encounters with them, the Catawbas were able to keep the alien people at arm's length. Colonial traders traveled up-country to the Catawbas' villages and Indian diplomats headed in the opposite direction to visit colonial capitals, but until the mid-1700s the Nation's location spared it daily encounters with large numbers of foreigners. The Catawbas' isolation was vital to their ultimate survival, for it gave them time to adjust to the newcomers before having to come face to face with farmers, the most serious threat Europeans posed.

Unlike the traders and diplomats with whom the Catawbas were accustomed to dealing, farmers had no use for the Indians. Colonial traders needed Indian hunters to stay in business, and Crown diplomats needed Indian war-

riors to protect their country. Hence traders and diplomats had worked hard to keep Catawbas happy and thriving. But settlers did not need the Indians—not as hunters, not as warriors, not as anything—and therefore had no interest in protecting them. To the settlers, Indians were in the way.

Catawbas had been spared these unfriendly neighbors for a long time because there was still plenty of land attractive to settlers along the coast. After the Yamasee War of 1715, however, colonists looking for good farmland began to venture beyond the coastal plain to the Piedmont's rolling hills and rich soil. During the 1730s farmers moved into the lands of the Wateree tribe in central South Carolina and by 1750 a few venturesome people were approaching the Catawbas' six villages at the junction of Sugar Creek and the Catawba River. There this influx of

A 1750 map showing the main trade route (lightly dotted lines) between Charles Town (Charleston) and the Catawbas' villages at the junction of Sugar Creek and the Catawba River. Although it is not labeled on the map, the Catawba River is the upper branch of the Wateree River.

homesteaders coming upriver met another coming down from Pennsylvania and Virginia, and together they quickly populated the area of the Carolina Piedmont. By 1755 the Catawbas were surrounded and outnumbered. Five hundred families lived within 30 miles of the Indians, and land surveyors busily measuring out more farms were marching right through the Indians' villages.

In our age of interstate highways, road maps, and motel chains it is difficult to imagine what it was like to be a colonist moving into the Piedmont frontier in the 18th century. To the early settler the highways were twisting trails, the road maps only rumors of routes, the motels whatever shelter could be thrown together from the bark, branches, and earth that lay at hand. In his old age Robert Witherspoon, who as a child in the 1730s had moved into an area southeast of the Catawbas, still vividly remembered those first scary days. "My mother and us children were still in expectation that we were coming to an agreeable place, but when we arrived and saw nothing but a wilderness and instead of a fine timbered house, nothing but a very mean dirt house, our spirits quite sunk." Even after the family got used to frontier life, according to Witherspoon, they "were still opprest with fears on diverse accounts, especially of being massacred by the Indians or bit by the snakes or being lost or perished in the woods." To the inexperienced homesteader the Indians, with their strange looks, strange ways, and strange speech, were as frightening as poisonous snakes or the dark forest itself. Even settlers who lived at some distance from the Catawbas' villages saw Indians, for on hunting expeditions Indians would sweep across a colonial settlement like "Egyptian locusts," as one settler wrote. Catawbas, of course, saw things differently. To them it was the intruders who seemed like locusts, swarming over the Indians' homeland.

Although they did not particularly like each other, neither side was actually interested in starting a war. The settlers were more concerned with making a new life in a new land than they were in exterminating natives. For their part, the Catawbas knew too well the consequences of battling colonists and were eager to avoid the mistake they had made in the Yamasee War. Nonetheless, it was not long before fighting broke out, caused mainly by what one South Carolina official termed "the difference of manners and way of life" between Indian and European. This difference took several forms. Settlers felt that there was plenty of room in this new land, and that in any case Indians did not own it. Catawbas disagreed and drove off anyone who settled on land too close to the Nation. Settlers believed in private property and put up fences to mark their lands. Catawbas believed that no person could claim land forever and tore the fences down. Catawbas thought it was perfectly acceptable to roam across the countryside in search of game. Settlers considered the Indian

hunters to be trespassers and wrecked their camps. Catawbas subscribed to a belief in hospitality, providing all visitors with food and drink. Settlers looked upon an Indian who dropped by for a meal as a beggar, and they called a native who took what settlers refused to give him a thief.

Other clashes occurred because the two peoples were too much alike. They fought over livestock, for example. The Indians had begun keeping cattle around 1750, and they as well as the settlers let their horses and cattle wander through the woods to find their own food, which made every animal an easy target for thieves—Indian or non-Indian. Catawbas and colonists were also very fond of liquor, and drunkenness was, as Hagler pointed out, "the very Cause" of many of the crimes each side committed against the other.

The Catawbas and colonists were acting out a familiar plot. In all of Britain's American colonies the story was similar: After settlers moved near to Indians, trouble soon followed. The ending was also predictable, with Indians all too often fleeing west or standing firm, fighting, and being exterminated. Only a few of the many tribes living in the East when Europeans first arrived managed to avoid one or the other of these fates. If Catawbas were to become one of the few survivors, they would have to be less obstinate. Instead of fighting the intruders, they would have to find some way of living with them.

That search took the Indians in several directions, and they ended up mak-

A Catawba cane basket. Household items handcrafted by the Catawbas were in high demand among the settlers, and some Indian women traveled as far away as Charleston to sell the wares they made.

ing friends in various ways. They started a brisk trade with settlers in household goods made by Catawba women. The Indians had not totally lost their knowledge of their traditional crafts, and they now turned these skills into a profitable business. Leather moccasins and baskets or mats made of cane were widely sought, but pottery was by far the most popular item. As early as 1772, Catawba women were going from house to house peddling their crafts to local farmers. These goods, manufactured in the same way by generations of Catawbas, were in such great demand that by 1800, Indian women were traveling all the way to Charleston to sell their products. Some settlers believed that certain dishes such as okra soup should only be cooked in Catawba

pots, for these vessels alone gave the soup its full flavor. Besides the financial profits from this business, which were particularly important because the Indians' income from the deerskin trade had declined to almost nothing, the pottery trade was significant because it now made Catawbas valuable to settlers. The farmers now looked upon Indians less as trespassers or beggars than as peddlers of useful wares.

The Catawbas' image and their income were also enhanced by the land itself. In 1763, Catawbas had asked for and received title to 144,000 acres of land—a tract approximately 15 miles square—from the king of England. This reservation did not give the Indians all of the territory they claimed, which amounted to most of the Carolina Piedmont. But because a smallpox outbreak in 1759 had reduced their numbers from 2,500 to fewer than 1,000—and from 6 villages to 1—there were no longer enough Indians to make an effective claim to their entire homeland. Title to this reservation gave them the core of their territory along the Catawba River and helped them protect it from invasion by colonists. When settlers ventured onto Indian land, Catawba leaders would pull out the title outlining the boundary the trespassers had crossed. If that did not work, the Catawbas could complain to the authorities, who were obligated to try to enforce the king's laws.

Enforcing these laws on the frontier was never easy, however. Before long the Catawbas realized that it was more

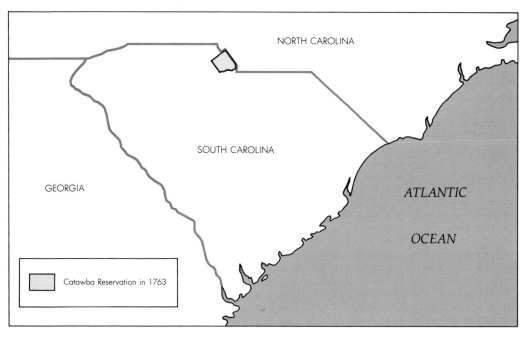

profitable and more diplomatic to rent their reservation land to settlers. The Catawbas' first tenant, Thomas Spratt, leased several thousand acres of the reservation from the Nation's leaders in the 1760s. Soon many other settlers followed suit. By 1800 several hundred white families had negotiated with the Nation's leaders and set up farms on Catawba land. These tenants paid an annual rent in cash, clothing, or livestock. Although the Catawbas were reluctant to invite this invasion of their homeland, they had little choice. The Indians needed the money, and their white neighbors were eager to have more farmland. Renting land brought the Indians an income, satisfied the settlers' desire for more farmland, and—as with the sale of pottery—gave Ca-

tawbas a better image. To the settlers Catawbas were no longer dangerous hunters and warriors but friendly landlords and potters.

To these two new titles Catawbas added another that was, in the long run, even more important to their survival: that of patriots. When the American colonies declared their independence from Great Britain in 1776, Catawbas gave their full support to the rebel cause. During the American Revolution Catawba warriors fought alongside American troops at many battles throughout the South. The Indians who remained at home provided food to hungry patriots. South Carolinians were deeply grateful to the Catawbas for having, as one prominent Camden merchant put it, "taken so noble a part

On August 16, 1780, British forces defeated American troops at the Battle of Camden, about 50 miles south of the Catawbas' villages. The Catawbas actively supported the American Revolution both at home and at the front, providing food as well as warriors to the Continental army.

[in the war] and . . . fought and Bled with your white Brothers of America."

With the defeat of the British the Catawbas were careful to tailor their political system to fit the new American nation. During the American Revolution, when the Catawba chief "King" Frow (all chiefs were called "King" in colonial records) abdicated, the Catawba leaders selected a warrior named New River to take his place. The Catawbas addressed this new leader as "general" rather than "king." In a land where *General* George Washington had just led the revolt against *King* George III, this was a shrewd decision. Although New River and later chiefs continued, as always, to be chosen on the basis of their descent from earlier chiefs, the Catawbas downplayed this similarity to the British monarchy, stressing instead the council's role in selecting the leader, which was in fact nothing new. Surrounded by a society that took great pride in its democratic system, it was good public relations for Catawbas to pretend that they, too, had overthrown a king and voted in a new leader.

The Catawba Nation's campaign to win the hearts of its neighbors was further helped by Indians who served as informal goodwill ambassadors to the neighboring settlers. One such person was Peter Harris, who had been orphaned by the smallpox epidemic of 1759 and raised by Thomas Spratt, the first white man to lease the Catawbas' land. Harris eventually returned to his people, but he was never away from the Spratts for long. He regaled the family with stories of his exploits in the revolutionary war and his brief stage career in England, where he had toured theaters with several other Catawba warriors, performing their war dances and singing traditional songs. In the early 1820s, when his health failed, the elderly Harris returned to the Spratt farm to be cared for. It was then that he asked to be buried in the Spratt family graveyard, where a marker to this Indian, long a friend to the whites, still stands.

On his many visits with the Spratts, Peter Harris probably crossed paths with Sally New River, another Catawba who advanced the Nation's friendly relations with its white neighbors. The granddaughter of Hagler and wife of New River, she enjoyed the respect of her people and the affection of local whites. When visitors arrived unannounced, it was Sally New River who made sure they were fed. After her hus-band's death in 1804 she spent months at a time with the Spratts. But she was well known to many people in the area. On occasion she would have a drink in a local tavern and perhaps tease a newcomer who was afraid of snakes. At other times she listened politely as her white friends tried to correct her broken English or pleaded with her to ride her horse like a proper lady. Fifty years after her death around 1820, local whites were still recalling "old aunt Sally" with affection.

These informal ambassadors, along with the Indians' reputation as potters and patriots, helped Catawbas fit in. Still, the settlers' more favorable impression of the Catawbas was no guarantee that the Nation's future would be prosperous or secure. Rents from reservation lands were not enough to feed and clothe the Indians, especially when tenants fell behind in their payments. Some tenants went even further and abused their Indian landlords. Around 1800, for example, Thomas Spratt became angry with General New River and according to Spratt family tradition began "banging 'Old New River' with a pole all over the yard." There had been a time, not too long before, when Spratt would not have lived to tell this tale. But by 1800 the Catawbas were too outnumbered to fight back in the old way, and they lacked the weapons to fight the settlers on their own terms. The Catawbas could not bring a suit against a tenant who owed rent or a settler who committed a crime. Indians, like blacks, were

*A 19th-century engraving of slaves operating a cotton press. Although blacks had been mem-
bers of de Soto's expedition, fought in the Yamasee War, and traded with the Indians, by
1800, many Catawbas, like most whites, considered blacks to be inferior.*

forbidden by law from giving testimony
in a courtroom.

"Like blacks"—the very words
struck fear into the heart of the Nation
and represented one of the greatest
threats to the Indians' future. After
1800, cotton became the southern Piedmont's main crop, and plantations
worked by black slaves surrounded the
Catawbas' territory. The Indians now
found themselves the third race in a
South that tended to see people only as
black or white. In this color-conscious
society, anyone with dark skin was in
danger of being classified as "colored."
When it came to granting rights, such
as testifying in court, serving on juries,
voting, or holding office, officials of
South Carolina drew a clear line that
divided whites from Indians, blacks, or
mulattos (persons of mixed ancestry).
Local whites had the same tendency as
the state officials to lump Catawbas
with blacks. When two Indians visited
a church near the reservation they were
told by someone there that "white

people come to my church. Indians cannot come to church here. Go to church with the colored people." No wonder the Catawbas were said by one white observer to "live . . . in obsessed fear of being regarded as 'colored' and classified with negroes."

The Indians feared being classified as "colored" because this represented a loss of their Indian identity, as well as because of the clearly disadvantaged status that was attached to it. The Catawba response to this threat to their identity took several forms. Their first step was to distance themselves from blacks more than ever before. In colonial times the Indians had thought of blacks in much the same way as they thought of whites. Some of the first blacks the Indians had met, for example, were explorers in de Soto's party, traders with the Nation, and soldiers in the Yamasee War. But by 1800, blacks were clearly slaves, and the Catawbas realized that if they were to avoid a similar fate they would have to emphasize to whites their distinctness. They would have to begin treating blacks as inferiors. And they did, echoing the whites' racist rhetoric and even buying a few black slaves themselves.

Another way for Catawbas to distance themselves from blacks was to remain identifiably Indian. Despite all the changes in their way of life, no Catawba in the early 19th century was likely to be mistaken for a white—or black—person. Even though they dressed like their neighbors, they also wore silver nose rings, some with tiny silver hearts

dangling from them. They might live in log cabins and sit on chairs, but they still had no tables, preferring to eat from a common tub set on the cabin floor. Although they might speak English and have English names, they knew Catawba far better and used Indian names among themselves.

The clearest sign of the Indians' refusal to give up their habits, however, was their continuing indifference to Christianity. European settlers tried various methods to convert the Catawbas, but to no avail. Just before the American Revolution the College of William and Mary in Williamsburg, Virginia, had admitted John Nettles, a Catawba youth. He spent three years there learning English ways. Nettles returned to his people carrying a Bible, but he could not persuade anyone to embrace the message it conveyed. Until his death around 1812 the man the settlers called "the educated Indian" remained a curiosity among his people.

A Baptist minister named Jacob Rooker had no more success than Nettles did. Just after 1800 Rooker set up a school and a church on the reservation, but after only a few years he had to close his mission because the Indians stopped coming. The settlers were furious with the Catawbas' refusal to change. "These wretched Indians," wrote one settler in 1826, "though they live in the midst of an industrious people, . . . will be Indians still."

Meanwhile the Nation's tenants were also becoming frustrated, although for different reasons. They wanted to own, not rent, the Catawba land that they had been farming for years. Around 1830 they began asking the South Carolina state legislature—which now met in Columbia, having moved from Charleston just after the revolutionary war—to buy the land from the Indians. Throughout the 1830s the legislature sent representatives to negotiate the sale of the Catawbas' land, but the Indians were reluctant to give up their homeland. Although they now numbered only about 100 people and rented almost every scrap of the reservation to settlers, they still felt that this land had always been theirs and should remain theirs forever. Here were the sites of their ancient villages, the ruins still visible among the trees. Here lay the bones of their ancestors in a patch of bottomland along the east side of the Catawba River known as "King's Bottom." Living on this sacred ground, the elders stood firm against the tides pushing for sale. These men were the last of the Catawba warriors. They had fought the Iroquois and the British, they had known General New River and Thomas Spratt. Their roots in the past were deep, and they would not change their minds.

Time was against them, however. One by one the old men died, until by the end of the 1830s all were gone. In their place stood a new generation of leaders, younger Catawbas with a different vision of the Nation's future. These younger men, feeling the pressure from settlers, wanted to sell the Catawbas' land and use the proceeds to

On March 13, 1840, the Catawbas signed the Treaty of Nation Ford. In this treaty the Indians agreed to give up their reservation along the Catawba River in exchange for a new tract of land in a less populated area. The Catawbas were also promised $2,500 upon leaving their reservation and $1,500 a year for nine years afterward.

make a new life for themselves elsewhere. In the 1830s U.S. government policy favored the removal of eastern Indians to the West, where no settlers yet clamored for land. Following this policy, between 1830 and 1850 the government forcibly removed thousands of Indians to lands across the Mississippi

River. What is now the state of Oklahoma was then known as Indian Territory. To it went Seminole, Cherokee, Creek, and other eastern Indians. Some Catawbas felt that they, too, should relocate to western lands. Others favored selling the reservation and using the money to buy land in a more remote part of the Carolinas where they might have some peace. Whatever direction the Nation took, its new leaders wanted to sell the reservation.

The sale of the Catawbas' reservation took place in the spring of 1840 at Nation Ford, a crossroads overlooking the Catawba River. The Treaty of Nation Ford stipulated that the Catawbas relinquish to the state of South Carolina their 144,000 acres of land. In return, the state promised to use $5,000 to buy land elsewhere in a place of the Indians' choosing or, if that was not possible, to give the Indians $5,000 in cash. In addition, the Nation would receive another $2,500 in cash when it left its homeland. The state also agreed to pay the Catawba Nation $1,500 a year for nine years. On March 13, the two sides signed the treaty, and the South Carolinians thought they had seen the last of the Catawbas.

It did not work out that way. The plan to resettle beyond the Mississippi River fell through, even though the federal government pledged to add $5,000 to the money the Indians had been promised by the state to help pay their way. Other Indians recently removed to the West did not want Catawbas to join them, because they would have had to share land as well as government payments and services. Few Catawbas wanted to go west anyway. Efforts to buy an out-of-the-way spot of land in the Carolinas also failed. With nowhere else to go, many Catawbas joined the 1,000 Cherokees who had avoided removal in North Carolina. But these old foes could not get along, and by the end of the 1840s the Catawbas who had settled there wanted to leave.

One band of Catawbas remained along the Catawba River, living on a reservation of 630 acres that the state of South Carolina purchased for them in 1841. The state's leaders had hoped that the Indian men would become farmers on this land and follow the example of white men. The state supplied the Indians with farm equipment and advice, and an agent employed by the state administered the program. But by 1843 the project had failed, and the tiny tract along the west side of the Catawba River sat almost empty.

The Treaty of Nation Ford all but destroyed the Catawba Nation. "We have no home. . . ," the Catawbas said in a petition to the South Carolina legislature in 1844, "we feel lost without a home." And lost they were. Those Catawbas still living in South Carolina and those living with the Cherokee in North Carolina were said to be disorganized and leaderless. "As a Nation," South Carolina governor David Johnson said of the Catawbas in 1847, "they are, in effect, dissolved." But Johnson was wrong—this was not the end of the Catawba Nation. ▲

Frank Cantey, photographed by Frank G. Speck in 1929.

CATAWBA ELDERS
AND
MORMON ELDERS

When Governor Johnson proclaimed the end of the Catawba Nation in 1847, he was not the first person to state that the Catawbas were extinct or predict that they soon would be. A century earlier Governor James Glen had worried about "the Total destruction of that poor Nation," and another observer had left the Nation in 1754 "perswaided that the Catawba Nation will be no more in one Year's Time." In the mid-19th century others besides Johnson were convinced that the Catawbas would soon be extinct as a people and, as one South Carolinian wrote, "the last sod will be thrown on . . . [the Nation's] grave."

All of these authorities were wrong. Toward the end of the 1840s the Catawbas, who had been homeless since the Treaty of Nation Ford in 1840, began to drift back to the lands of their ancestors,

to the banks of the Catawba River. By 1850 more than 100 Indians had returned and were huddled on and around the tiny reservation of 630 acres that the state had bought for them in 1841. This tract, small as it was, nonetheless was vital to the Nation's survival, for it gave the Indians a haven, a place they could cling to in good times and bad.

Once they had returned to the lands of their ancestors, the Catawbas set about preserving as much as they could of their ancestral ways. The best means of doing this was to teach the Nation's children the Catawba culture so they could carry it on into the future. Thus Indians growing up on the reservation between 1850 and 1880 received a "traditional" education. Their tutors were elderly members of the Nation, people who were born in the early part of the

The site of Old Town, a former Catawba settlement on a hill overlooking the Catawba River, is visible in the distance in this 1918 photograph. Although after 1840 the Catawbas no longer had title to their ancient territory, they continued to visit the land where their ancestors had lived.

19th century and were well versed in the traditional lore. The language of instruction was invariably Catawba. A visitor to the Nation in 1856 discovered that Catawba children spoke only Catawba until they were at least 10 or 12 years old. Many who were much older than that still had not learned English. Knowledge of their ancestral tongue was important, for it opened avenues to the Catawba past for the children. At the same time, their ignorance of English closed off avenues for learning about the world from outsiders whose values and ways were different.

The elderly Catawba teachers instilled their knowledge not through formal classroom lessons but through demonstrating everyday skills and telling stories that educated while they entertained. Robert Harris, born in 1867, was one of the children taught by this method. In later years he recalled "how it was understood by the Catawba of a generation ago that story-telling was intended to develop the mind, to make children think, to teach them the ways of life."

The lessons covered a variety of subjects. History was vitally important. Catawba tales recounted battles with such Indian tribes as the Shawnee, the Chickasaw, and the Tuscarora. These Indians had been terrifying foes, but in the end the Catawbas always won. One Catawba story ended, "Whenever the Shawnee came they were killed." One victim of the Shawnee raiders, Hagler, stood out among the heroes of these old wars. "They still speak of him with much feeling," wrote one observer in the mid-19th century. Catawbas continued to visit his grave near the Catawba River to pay their respects to this revered leader. Other important historic sites where a child could come in close touch with his people's past included the locations of the villages along the Catawba River where "the ancient people" had lived. Among the Catawbas the past lived alongside the present, and this constant emphasis on a close

connection helped give the children a sense of their distinctive Indian identity.

Through Catawba elders the knowledge of the ancient Indians was passed on to the young people of a new generation. By watching, listening, and doing, Catawba girls learned how to make a pot or cook parched-corn soup. Boys watched their elders and were

Margaret Brown, photographed in 1913 as she worked on a piece of pottery. She and other Catawbas born in the late 19th century were the last generation to receive a traditional education through the instruction of their elders.

A Catawba man and boy practice using a blowgun, the Indians' traditional weapon for hunting birds. By watching and imitating their elders, Catawba children learned the skills they would later need as adults.

given the opportunity to practice the old arts of trapping fish in baskets made of white-oak splints or hunting birds by torchlight. These skills and others tied young Catawbas to the wisdom of the past while helping them live in the present and prepare for the future.

Another important skill was medicine. Although in the 19th century the Catawbas no longer had an official religious healer as they had had in the past, much of the medical lore developed by earlier healers was still known and used. For instance, several plants could be used to heal backaches, and a rattlesnake skin bound around the head was sure to give relief from a headache. No less important than the right prescription was the way in which the cure was carried out. Catawbas had rules for when and how to gather the herbs that went into making medicines. It was important that the plant be picked during a new or full moon and no less important that while harvesting these potions the person pray to ''He-Who-Never-Dies'' (God) for help. Without such precautions, no medicine, no matter how potent, could work its cure.

The old people also had the answers to questions that naturally curious children ask about the world they live in: Where do storms come from? How does water flow? How did the chipmunk get his stripes, the opossum his strange grin and hairless tail, and the robin his red breast? The Catawba elders told stories that answered all of these questions and others as well. Their tales, prayers, and examples all helped raise the Nation's children as Catawbas and all ensured that the wisdom of the ages would live on.

Much about these 19th-century teachers and their lessons is known because one person talked at length with their students. This man was Frank G. Speck, an anthropologist from the University of Pennsylvania, who in the first half of the 20th century spent a great deal of time among the small tribes living in the eastern United States. Speck first visited the Catawbas in 1913, and

A Catawba man demonstrates the practice of blowing herb medicine into a medicine pot in the early 1900s. The Catawbas continued to use the remedies developed by their religious healers into the 20th century, long after the last man who held the title had died.

he returned to the reservation frequently until his death in 1950. On each visit Speck sought out those Catawbas who could tell him something about the old ones and their ways. Speck was especially interested in finding out what he could about the ancient Catawbas— the words, tools, stories, and values that might be hundreds or even thousands of years old. He was sometimes disappointed, because the Catawba language had borrowed many words from English, and some so-called "ancient" tales had as their main characters not rabbits or snapping turtles, traditional animals in Indian lore, but pigs, which had been introduced by Europeans. The new words, animals, and values Speck uncovered were signs of the Catawbas' flexibility, their ability to change to meet the needs of the times. The changes that Speck identified and was disappointed in are integral clues to understanding the Catawbas' survival in a changing world.

Speck, who learned to speak Catawba, was the first to write down for future generations these traditional Catawba stories as they were told him. He was also the last, because the Catawbas born before about 1880 were the last children to grow up in the traditional manner. As Speck himself noted in 1934, "The younger Indians are a different people from those even of their parents' generation." Others had noticed the difference long before Speck did. In 1893, elderly Catawbas on the reservation were complaining that "Our people are getting out of the old

A group of Catawba children, photographed by anthropologist Frank G. Speck in 1922. Through his interviews with older Catawbas, Speck hoped to preserve what remained of the Indians' traditional folklore so that future generations could learn about the ways and beliefs of the Catawbas.

ways and the young folks take no interest in what our fathers used to do."

The first sign of disinterest was the loss of the Catawba language. By the turn of the century only a minority of the Indians still spoke their own tongue fluently. By the time Speck got there, only a handful could tell him the old tales in the old tongue. "[T]hey isn't more then 10 or 12 that can speak it now," Leola Blue, a Catawba woman, wrote to him in 1919. "The young set of people Just dont try to learn it they speak English all to gather."

To his dismay, Speck discovered that except for pottery the old crafts were also dying out. Although the number of people who practiced these skills had been in decline since the early 1700s, the crafts had never really disappeared totally. Now, however, the bow and arrow, which Catawba men had still made and used in the 19th century, was increasingly scarce, as were everyday household utensils made the traditional way. Leola Blue did her best to get some examples of these crafts for Speck in the fall of 1919, but she had little success. "[A]ll of the old people who made such as baskets spoons an all those Kind of things are all dead now," she wrote to Speck at the end of the year, "an the younger people never trys to learn to make such things now[.]" In Blue's fruitless search were the signs of a dying cultural tradition. The old dances and ceremonies, like the spoons and baskets or the words and stories, were now a thing of the past.

The crucial link between generations had been broken; children no longer followed quite so closely in their parents' footsteps. There were several reasons for this relatively sudden break in the chain connecting one generation to the next. The first was the arrival of Charles Roberson and Henry Miller in May 1883. Roberson and Miller were elders (leaders) from the Church of Jesus Christ of Latter-Day Saints, or Mormon church. This religion, which was founded in the early 19th century by Joseph Smith, was headquartered in Salt Lake City, Utah. Although missionaries had come to the Nation before, all had failed to convert the Catawbas to Christianity. But Roberson, Miller, and Mormon missionaries who followed them were to experience both greater hardship and greater success.

A Catawba demonstrates how pottery is made. The clay is rolled into cylinders, which are coiled, one on top of the other, to form the sides of the pot. Then the sides are thinned and evened out by scraping and rubbing the vessel with a stone. After the pot dries, it is ready to be fired in an outdoor pit or fireplace. Firing hardens the clay and produces a watertight vessel.

Nearby whites considered Mormonism a dangerous and unchristian new sect—at the time it permitted a man to have more than one wife and seemed to some to contradict the Bible's teachings. The local whites tried their best to drive the missionaries away. In 1884 a mob stormed the reservation where they caught and whipped Mormon missionary Franklin A. Fraughton. Fraughton's partner barely escaped, fleeing into the woods in a hail of gunfire. Although mobs made other Mormon missionaries promise never to return to the reservation, replacements always showed up, and the Indians always welcomed them. In November 1883 the first 5 Indians were baptized, and within a year there were 20 converts and a Sunday school on the reservation. After the mob whipping in 1884, meetings often had to take place in secret, out of sight of opponents, but this did not slow the missionaries' progress. By 1900 more than 75 percent of the Catawba Nation had converted to Mormonism.

The Mormon religion had much to do with convincing the Catawbas, who had been indifferent to missionaries for 200 years, to give up their traditional religious beliefs. Mormonism gave American Indians a special place. *The Book of Mormon*, one of the religion's holy books, purported to be an account of the Indians' ancestors. It predicted that they could become "a white and delightsome people" if they accepted church teachings. At the same time, Mormon scripture said that those upon whom "the Lord God did cause a skin of blackness to come" were "an idle people, full of mischief." Although *The Book of Mormon* was not referring specifically to the black population of the American South, the missionaries' message was interpreted by many Catawbas as giving spiritual reinforcement to their attitudes toward Afro-Americans. Thus to the Catawbas the Mormon doctrine encouraged their efforts to distance themselves from blacks while at the same time supporting their desire to become more like whites, a course

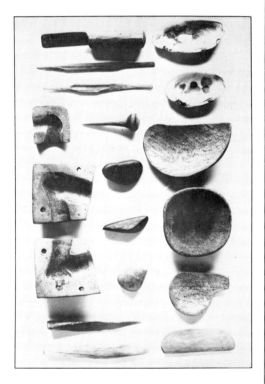

Among the Catawbas' traditional pottery-making tools are pipe molds (left), stones (center), cane (center, top), and mussel shells (right).

they had already been following for many years.

Mormonism changed Catawba life forever. For one thing, it divided the Nation geographically: Some Catawba believers moved west to Utah and Colorado to be near the center of their religion, while others remained in South Carolina. Those who stayed received from their new religion a set of values that, though not always opposed to what their ancestors had taught, nonetheless came from outside the Nation. These values stressed that it was the Indians' destiny to become whites. The power of this message was further strengthened because the Mormon way was all-encompassing. It was not just a matter of going to church on Sundays; converts embraced a faith that condemned the use of alcohol and tobacco and stressed hard work, individual improvement, and community spirit. As Mormonism became more accepted in the area, the Catawbas established clubs to teach these lessons to all ages. Thus Mormonism became the focal point of Catawba life. Now there was an alternative source of proper values, correct behavior, and tribal identity on the reservation that first competed with and ultimately replaced the Catawbas' traditional beliefs. Catawbas today, 90 percent of whom are Mormon, date the 1880s and the introduction of Mormonism as a significant turning point in the history of their people.

An important aspect of the Mormon program was formal education. Thus, by instilling in Indians a fervent desire

The Ladies Relief Society, one of many organizations Mormon missionaries established among the Catawbas to help instill the religion's teachings, photographed outside the Mormon church in the early 1900s.

for schooling, the Mormon religion also contributed to the Catawbas' disenchantment with the old ways. Although as early as 1801, Catawba leaders had asked the state of South Carolina to provide people to teach some of the Nation's children to read and write English, the state had not responded. Until the beginning of the 20th century the majority of Catawbas were illiterate, except for John Nettles and a few oth-

Children at the Carlisle Indian School in Pennsylvania learn the concept of fractions by folding a piece of paper into smaller parts. Carlisle was one of several boarding schools established in the 19th century to instill in Indian children the values of white American society, not only by classroom instruction but also by removing them from their homes and thus keeping them from learning the traditions of their people.

ers. Many states during the late 19th century had laws requiring white children and black children to attend separate schools. Because whites believed that Indians were inferior, schools for white children were closed to Indians. Schools for black children were either nonexistent or out of the question for the Catawbas, who stood the risk of being classified as black if they attended them. A few Catawba children attended Indian boarding schools in other states, where they were taught English, writing, arithmetic, and vocational skills such as farming or cooking. The aim of these schools was to distance Indians

from their traditional ways and expose them to the values of white society. By 1895 at least two Catawba girls had attended the Carlisle Indian School in Carlisle, Pennsylvania. Upon the completion of their studies there, students were expected to live with a rural white family for three years, working as farmhands or helping with domestic chores and becoming further acculturated, learning more of the customs of the mainstream, non-Indian, culture.

It was not until 1897 that a schoolteacher held classes on the Catawba reservation. That year the Presbyterian church sent Mrs. D. Eli Dunlap to es-

(continued on page 89)

COILED CLAY OF CAROLINA

A ceremonial wedding vase. Traditionally such containers were filled with perfume and placed in the bridal chamber on the wedding night.

For at least 4,000 years the Indians of southeastern North America have made pottery, and Catawba women have done so for at least 400 years. The tribe's men and children dig the clay from pits near their traditional territory in South Carolina. The women then clean the clay and grind it into a fine powder. They mix it with water and knead it to a puttylike consistency. Then it is ready to use.

To start, the potter shapes a lump of clay into a smooth, round pancake shape to form a base. More clay is rolled into short, ropelike cylinders. The potter begins to build the sides of the pot by coiling one of the cylinders around the base and smoothing the joint. She continues to add coils of clay, one on top of the other, blending each cylinder into the previous one to form a smooth surface inside and out. The pot is allowed to dry for a day or two, and then the potter thins and smoothes its walls. She wets the surface and adds moist clay to fill cracks and holes, using traditional tools such as polished bones, mussel shells, cane, and iron knives. She dampens the pot once more and polishes it with a smooth stone to remove any marks made in scraping. A potter's tools are highly valued and are often passed down from generation to generation. The pot is then left to dry in the sun or dried further in a warming oven before being fired (exposed to extreme heat) in an outdoor pit or open fireplace. Firing hardens the clay and makes the pot watertight. It also produces the orange, red, brown, black, or mottled colors for which Catawba pottery is noted.

The Catawba women who continue to make pottery using the traditional techniques are an ongoing link with the tribe's past. They ensure that Catawba pottery will remain the oldest art form still produced in South Carolina.

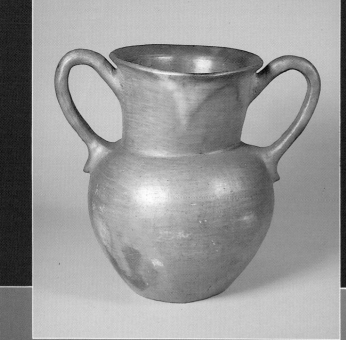

Left: *The black interior of this vase was created by placing sawdust or wood chips inside to reduce the clay's exposure to oxygen during the firing process.* **Below:** *Mottled vase with snake, made by Doris Blue in 1978. The clay figure was attached to the pot before firing.*

The mottling on this vase occurred during firing, when wood was heaped over and burned directly on the pot.

A two-handled vase, probably made early in the 20th century.

The Indian-head handles on this tripod bowl were shaped separately in a mold and were attached to the pot before it was fired.

A bowl made by Earl Robbins in 1987. Although pottery has traditionally been a women's craft, a few men have recently started working in clay.

A two-headed canoe bowl made by Sara Ayers in 1979.

Left: *Shallow bowl with an incised floral design, made by Alberta Ferrell in 1973.* **Below:** *A tripod bowl made by Georgia Harris in 1986. Harris is one of about 10 Catawba women who learned the skill before 1930, when the traditional techniques were still taught by the Nation's elders.*

Left: *Pitcher made by Georgia Harris in 1986. Its polished, woodlike appearance was achieved by rubbing the vessel with a smooth stone.* **Below:** *Tripod cooking pot made by Sara Ayers.*

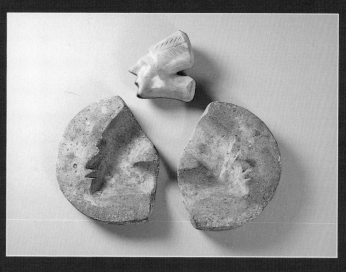

A pipe bowl and mold of fired clay designed in the shape of a face. The bowl is formed by pressing a cylinder of clay between the two halves of the mold.

A pipe bowl made in 1979.

A six-pronged bowl pipe made before 1920. Such pipes, known as friendship pipes, were passed among a group, and each person smoked from one of the prongs.

87

Catawbas began to make decorative pieces such as this turtle and frog only in the 20th century. Their earlier pieces were primarily functional cooking wares or pipes, which were popular trade items.

(continued from page 80)

tablish a school for Catawba children. She stayed for almost a decade, living in a house of her own on the reservation and teaching in a schoolhouse the Indians built for her. At one point she had 18 students in her "dear little Mission School," as she called it, and with her encouragement 7 more Catawba children attended the Carlisle Indian School.

Mrs. Dunlap's successes, however, were clouded by opposition. Many Catawbas wanted Mormons to teach them, not the Presbyterian Dunlap. The battle over Dunlap's presence raged for years, with some Indians plotting to run her off the reservation and others writing letters to the local newspaper in her defense. Dunlap eventually left the school, and in 1910 a Mormon teacher began holding classes on the reservation. Later the state of South Carolina took over the task of educating the Catawbas, appropriating $1,500 a year to run a public school on the reservation. Through the efforts of Mrs. Dunlap, the Mormons, and the state, Catawba children were introduced to a new world. Now, instead of sitting at the feet of their elders, they were sitting in a classroom. The language was English, the history was now centered on Europe and its colonies, and the world's ways were taught by civics and science textbooks, not folktales and prayers.

In addition to churches and schools, the growing number of marriages between Catawbas and whites was also an agent of change. These marriages defied the South's policy of segrega-tion, which tried to divide white from "colored" in all areas of life, in restaurants and restrooms, in trains and schools. A South Carolina law of 1879 forbidding marriages between whites and blacks or Indians posed no real problem, however. Indians and whites got around the law by finding a sympathetic official or by establishing a common-law marriage, in which the couple lived together without a formal marriage ceremony. At the same time, marriages between Indians and blacks were unheard of. A visitor to the reservation in 1893 reported, "They do not mix blood with the negroes, for whom they entertain the strongest antipathy." In 1919, Leola Blue informed Frank Speck, "they isn't over six now that are full Indians." Intermarriage changed the Catawbas' culture, as children were increasingly brought up according to white standards and values.

Thus in a few short years the combination of Mormonism, formal education, and mixed marriages had helped to weaken the grip of the ancient ways, the bond between old and young that had sustained Catawbas over the centuries. One Catawba man told Frank Speck that "some of them [Catawbas] now living, were when children frightened at meeting their grandparents on the road." The elders had once been sources of wisdom and objects of admiration. Now they were shunned as strangers.

For all the changes these forces brought to Catawba life, the Indians were still a long way from fulfilling the

A monument in Fort Mill, South Carolina, erected in 1900 to honor Catawbas who served in the Confederate army.

Mormon prophecy that they would become white. Although more than 20 Catawba men had fought for the South in the Civil War (1861–65), Catawbas still faced discrimination because of their race. Politically they were closer to blacks than to whites, being forbidden by law to vote or hold office. Economically, too, whites kept Catawbas out-

side the mainstream of American life. The development of the textile industry in the nearby city of Rock Hill, South Carolina, had not yet touched people on the reservation, who because of segregation laws and local racism were barred from working in the mills. Instead, Indians eked out a living doing a variety of jobs. Catawba women sold pottery and worked in cotton fields owned by whites. Most of their husbands, brothers, and sons sold firewood, hunted, and fished. To add to their diet everyone on the reservation gathered wild fruits and vegetables such as dandelion greens, wild plums, and wild onions. A few men became "professional Indians," dressing up in costumes and traveling to fairs and carnivals, where they demonstrated their skills with the bow and arrow. Robert Harris followed in the footsteps of his ancestor Peter Harris, the Catawba warrior who had traveled in Europe in the late 1700s. The younger Harris toured the country playing an Indian in the show "Daniel Boone on the Trail" and later played an Indian in a production of the Tennessee Opera Company.

None of these occupations earned Catawbas a very good living. At the end of the 19th century one observer ranked the Catawba income level below that of local blacks, who were themselves sunk in the depths of poverty. The Indians' houses were ramshackle and their crops poor. "Hungry time, have nothing, nakedness, have nothing," went one Catawba chant. "A poor person am I," said another. "I do not even have a shoe. . . . Somebody who has much money, some rich man, do give me money!"

Like other members of the Harris family, Ben P. Harris toured with a traveling show to earn income. He wears the type of clothing most often associated with American Indians, that of the Indians of the Great Plains region, which was not the Catawbas' traditional style of dress.

Even Catawbas who were financially secure found it impossible to overcome lingering white prejudice, as one Catawba woman discovered around 1910. She and her husband, an Iroquois Indian she had met when they were students at the Carlisle Indian School, lived in Rock Hill, where her husband worked as a railroad clerk. Here was a Catawba success story: educated Indians living and working among whites. Yet the story did not have a happy ending. When they tried to enroll their six-year-old daughter in a local school for white children, they were not allowed to do so. Unable to go to school with whites, unwilling to go to school with blacks, and too far from the reservation to go to school with other Indians, the girl was taught at home by a white tutor.

The dawn of the 20th century found the Catawbas a confused people: They were discriminated against, as black people were in South Carolina, even though they were not black. They had lost close contact with most of what made them immediately identifiable as Indians. But they were not white, either. As one white man asked, "If you're not an Indian, what are you?" Catawbas still did not know. ▲

Mrs. Sampson Owl, photographed by Frank G. Speck.

7

AN END
AND
A BEGINNING

During the 20th century, Catawbas have continued to wrestle with the question of who they are. In many ways they have moved steadily closer to the society that surrounds them and further away from their heritage. At the same time, however, they have never been able or willing to shed forever their Indian identity. This old tug-of-war between past and present, old and new, Indian and white has continued to define Catawba history and life to the present day.

In the first half of the century clear barriers continued to separate Catawbas from whites. One was the sheer poverty still prevalent on the reservation. In March 1930, the Indian agent for South Carolina, who administered state programs for the Catawbas, reported that most of the houses were one-room dwellings "with holes in the roof, sometimes with a family of six or eight living in the one little room."

Mixed with this grinding poverty was fierce pride, said to be inherited from the days when Catawba warriors were feared throughout the East. One local white noted in 1930 that though poor, "the Indian considers himself the equal of the white man and a white man is likely to get into trouble if he curses an Indian." Moreover, Catawbas were reluctant to accept charity. According to one white farmer, "[W]hen the Indian comes around . . . asking you to give him something to eat, he . . . doesn't want charity doled out to him, he wants to give you something in exchange."

To preserve their pride and ease their poverty, Catawbas began to create a better political system that could

A Catawba woman and her children sell pottery at a roadside stand around 1930. Because of racial prejudice, Catawbas, who were often classified as black, were unable to get good jobs. Many peddled pottery to help support their families.

speak—and speak loudly—on behalf of the Nation. Between 1880 and 1930 the office of chief had sometimes been vacant, and the council elected to assist him occasionally failed to meet. In the 1930s, however, the system was revived and refined to make it more effective. A chief, a committee chairman, two councilmen, and a secretary met regularly to discuss the Nation's affairs and carry the wishes of the people to the wider world.

A driving force behind the Catawbas' political revival was Samuel Blue, who served as chief from 1931 to 1938, 1941 to 1943, and again from 1956 to 1958. Even between these terms of office, Blue was the man most Catawbas and outsiders looked to as the Nation's leader. He was perfect for the job. As one of the last to receive a traditional Catawba education, Blue had a deep knowledge of his people's culture and was one of Frank Speck's key sources on the tribe's customs. Yet at the same time he was an early and devout convert to Mormonism. Perhaps most important of all, Blue was a shrewd diplomat. Chief Blue's knowledge of tribal lore and his friendliness to whites made him an important figure in the Indians' efforts to preserve their heritage and at the same time better their situation.

The skills of Samuel Blue and the Catawbas' improved political organization brought important changes in the Nation's relationship with the state and federal governments. South Carolina had never fully paid the Catawbas the amount it had agreed to in the treaty of 1840. At the end of the 19th century the state was disbursing only $800 a year to the tribe. In the 1930s it raised its annual appropriation to around $9,000 a year. Still, after the salaries of the state Indian agent, doctor, mortician, and schoolteacher were deducted from this amount, very little was left for the Catawbas. In an effort to find better support, the Catawbas began to explore the possibility of establishing relations with the federal government in Washington, D.C.

By the late 19th century, the U.S. government had become involved in the affairs of many tribes. Federal Indian agents employed by the Bureau of Indian Affairs went among various tribes to carry out the government's policies toward Indians and supervise the distribution of payments and goods promised the Indians in treaties. The Catawbas, however, like many small groups of eastern Indians, had been classified as wards of the state rather than of the United States. South Carolina alone had signed the Treaty of Nation Ford; South Carolina alone spent money to help the Nation; and South Carolina alone sent an agent to the reservation to oversee the Indians' affairs.

Catawbas, never wholly happy with this arrangement, had long tried to establish ties with the federal government. As early as 1782 a delegation of Catawbas traveled all the way to Philadelphia, then the U.S. capital, to ask the national government for help, only to be sent home to the care of South Carolina. Fourteen years later another party of Catawbas camped outside President George Washington's home at Mount Vernon, Virginia, hoping to get his assistance, but they were unsuccessful. In 1805 the leaders of the Nation sent a letter to President Thomas Jefferson asking for help. Repeatedly, they were told to go home, to take their complaints to the state. Now, in the early 20th century, they again approached the federal government.

This time the government in Washington was more willing to listen. On March 28, 1930, members of the Senate Committee on Indian Affairs opened hearings in Rock Hill to look into the Catawbas' situation. This turned out to be the first of many discussions involving not only the federal government and the Indians but also state officials and local citizens. After extensive negotiations, the Catawbas, the state of South Carolina, and the federal Bureau

Samuel Blue, who served three terms as chief of the Catawba Nation, photographed around 1930. Blue often wore clothing typical of the Indians of the Great Plains, such as feathered war bonnets, to match the popular stereotype of what an Indian looked like and thus call attention to his tribe.

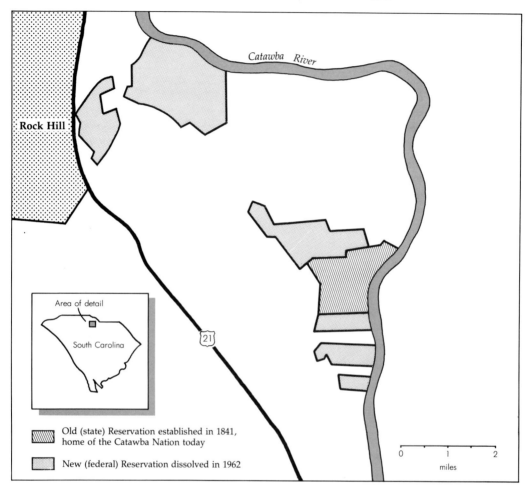

Area of detail

South Carolina

[21]

Catawba River

Rock Hill

Old (state) Reservation established in 1841, home of the Catawba Nation today

New (federal) Reservation dissolved in 1962

0   1   2
miles

of Indian Affairs signed a "Memorandum of Understanding" in 1943. In this three-way agreement South Carolina pledged to spend $75,000 to buy more reservation land for the Indians near the "Old Reservation," the small tract of 630 acres the state had bought for the Catawbas in 1841. The state also agreed to turn this "New Reservation" over to the federal government to ensure that it would be preserved for the Catawbas' use only. Lastly, South Carolina promised to admit the Indians to public schools and to make the Catawbas citizens of the state. (They had been citizens of the United States since 1924.)

On its part the federal government promised the Catawbas financial aid, medical assistance, and advice on making Indian businesses more profitable. The Catawbas in turn agreed to follow the recommendations of the Bureau of Indian Affairs and adopt a tribal constitution according to provisions of the Indian Reorganization Act (IRA) of

1934. The IRA gave Indian tribes the right to govern themselves and incorporate as businesses for the purpose of establishing profit-making enterprises. Through these means the framers of the IRA hoped that dying Indian cultures would be revitalized.

After 160 years of trying, the Catawbas were officially recognized as an Indian people by the government of the nation that their warrior ancestors had helped establish. Federal recognition affirmed their Indian identity and gave them the opportunity to qualify for certain benefits under U.S. laws. On June 30, 1944, the Catawbas adopted their new constitution and incorporated as the Catawba Indian Tribe of South Carolina. The bylaws established under the constitution provided for a tribal council composed of five officers: a chief, an assistant chief, a secretary-treasurer, and two trustees. The first meeting of the council took place in July 1944. Thereafter elections were held in July of even-numbered years. Any Catawba

A textile manufacturing plant in Fort Mill, South Carolina, around 1930. The Catawbas' gradual entry into the work force helped to break down stereotypes that many whites held about American Indians.

21 years of age or older was allowed to vote in tribal elections.

During the 1930s and 1940s, the Catawbas were in one sense becoming more Indian: Their reservation was six times larger, their government better established, their status as native Americans certified by the federal government. Ironically, they were at the same time heading in precisely the opposite direction—toward mainstream American society. There were several forces pushing them further in that direction than they had ever gone before.

First, in the late 1930s, several years before the state of South Carolina formally agreed to admit Indians to public schools, a few Catawbas began to attend the all-white high school in Rock Hill. They did so despite the segregation laws still in effect in the South at that time. For these young pioneers, life was often difficult. Forbidden by segregation laws to ride the school bus, the students had to catch rides from people on the reservation. At school they were subjected to the insults and taunts of their classmates. But the school superintendent, who had initiated their admission, stood behind them, and there was no organized effort to keep the Catawbas out. Another barrier had been broken down.

Many of the people who gave rides to Catawba students were other Catawbas on their way to work in the textile mills. Their entrance into the mills was the second major force that contributed to the Catawbas' acculturation. The textile boom that hit Rock Hill in the late

1800s had passed Catawbas by until 1918, when a Catawba man who had done farm work for one of the mill superintendents was given a mill job. But few Indians were allowed to follow him through the factory gates for another 20 years.

Reasons for white resistance varied. Some local whites hid behind segregation laws that prevented whites from hiring "coloreds" to explain their refusal to hire Indians. Other whites claimed that Indians "are not steady workers. Work per se doesn't appeal to them." To still others, Catawbas made poor workers because they were inferior, "like children" or "somewhat shiftless." Because of the Indians' pride, said another, "white people can't control them just like they would like to control a [black] laborer." Despite all these excuses for not employing Indians, Catawbas quietly persisted, and by 1940 this barrier, too, had been removed as one Catawba worker after another disproved the old stereotypes about them.

By bringing Catawbas and whites together more often than ever before, these new opportunities in business and education led to a dramatic increase in the rate of intermarriage after 1940. In 1958 one official reported that 120 out of 162 Catawba families contained one white spouse. With such a rate of intermarriage it is not surprising that "the old ones," people of solely Indian ancestry, fast disappeared. In 1954 Robert Lee Harris, said to be the last "full-blooded" Catawba man, died. Nine years later Hester Louise Cantey Blue, who claimed to be the last of the Nation's "full bloods," also died.

Even though after 1940 the Catawbas looked, talked, and acted more like their white neighbors, their legal status as Indians was more secure than ever. Given this situation, it is not surprising that the Nation suffered during these years from a clash of competing, contradictory value systems. On the one hand, traditional codes of conduct stressing cooperation, hospitality, and communal solidarity remained powerful and were expressed in a variety of ways. Voluntary labor, called "workings," was customary on the reservation, as neighbor helped neighbor in time of need. "When somebody builds something," one Catawba man explained, "everybody pitches in. I started building a home for my mother one morning, and by the end of the day 20 or 30 people were helping." The emphasis on cooperation meant that generosity was important; a person who had a little extra was expected to share, so that in the end everyone had about the same.

Against these enduring beliefs arose a new way of thinking derived from the outside world. This new social code stressed the individual more than the community, accumulation more than generosity. One Catawba described the new attitude as a "restlessness" that stemmed from "new ideas . . . the desire to see what other jobs and places were like." He dated its origins to the late 1930s, when schools and factories

were first beginning to open their doors to Indians.

With "restlessness" on the rise, conflict with the old ways was inevitable. Catawbas had often disagreed with one another, but during the 1950s and early 1960s the differences became more common and more bitter. Petty feuds— over a game of horseshoes, for example—became major conflicts. Indians who bought a new car or built a better house were the targets of jealous relatives and neighbors who called them "bigheaded" because they broke the rules about everyone staying the same. Not surprisingly, the number of cooperative activities declined. "Workings" became less common, social events would be planned but never take place. "It seems like they don't want to get together any more," one Catawba commented in the early 1960s.

While Catawbas squabbled among themselves they continued to have conflicts with whites. Local whites resented the Indians' efforts to gain equality. A school bus driver refused to pick up Catawba children; officials refused to let Indians register to vote. Some of this was racial prejudice, but some was resentment of Indians who wanted equality yet retained special privileges, such as government-provided medical care and exemption from property taxes, that came with federal recognition.

At the same time, the Nation's new relationship with the federal government was running into problems. The U.S. government attempted to set up an arts and crafts program to sell Ca-

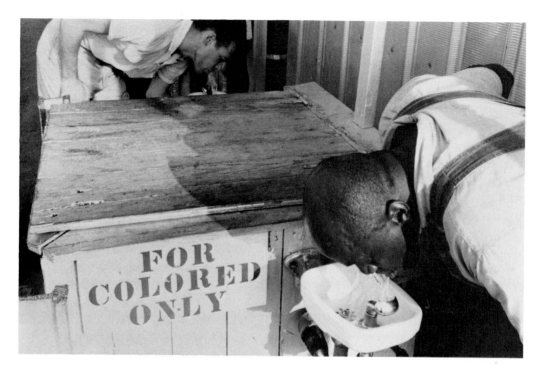

Along with blacks, Catawbas were often victims of segregation laws in southern states.

tawba pottery to tourists in South Carolina, but the project was unsuccessful. The Catawbas had never felt comfortable with the formal system of tribal government they had adopted in 1944. Some Catawbas resented the government's prohibition of the cutting of timber on the New Reservation, the land South Carolina had turned over to the federal government to manage. Several Catawbas continued to harvest firewood and Christmas trees in defiance of the regulations. "The Federal Government couldn't just come in and tell us what to do," one Indian said in the early 1960s. "We wouldn't toe the line for them." Still other Catawbas objected

to being unable legally to own their homes or lands because the land was held in trust by the government on behalf of the Indians.

The Catawbas' internal strife, their unhappiness with the federal government, and the local whites' resentment of them combined during the 1950s to push the Nation to accept the U.S. government policy of "termination." This policy, adopted by the government in the late 1940s, was designed to end American Indians' special status as sovereign nations within the United States. The policy was devised to end treaty obligations, dissolve tribal governments, and sell reservation lands—in short, to "terminate" tribes and absorb the Indians, one by one, into mainstream American life. Some proponents of this plan equated reservations with prison camps and promised to "liberate" the Indians. Others talked of ending the unfair "over-privileges" and "coddling" that they felt Indians enjoyed from the government. Opponents charged that termination violated sacred Indian treaty rights, destroyed Indian cultures, and served only to disguise another means by which whites stole Indian lands.

Catawbas were divided on termination. Led by Samuel Blue, those favoring it argued that breaking up the federally held reservation would give them deeds to their lands. This in turn would allow them to obtain loans so that they could improve their property. Blue and his followers were tired of being wards of the government; they wanted to be free to live their life as they saw fit, to pay taxes like all other citizens, and to, in the words of one Indian, "hold up their heads and look the world in the face." Those opposed wondered if the Nation was ready for such independence. Tax-free lands and free medical care were not to be given up without careful thought, especially when many Indians remained poor. They feared that once a Catawba had land he or she would sell it, not improve it, and the New Reservation would be crowded with strangers.

The issue finally came to a head on March 28, 1959, when the tribal council met in the schoolhouse on the Old Reservation, the state-owned land that would not be affected by the federal program of termination. By a vote of 40 to 17, Catawbas agreed to end their status as a federally recognized Indian tribe. After compiling a roll of tribal members totaling 631 people and setting aside land on which the school, church, and playground stood, the rest of the reservation was divided among the Catawbas. Each person had the choice of selecting a plot or receiving a percentage of the proceeds from the sale of whatever land was left after everyone who wanted a plot had chosen one. About 60 percent of the people chose to take land and were given title to it. The rest received cash from the land sale, which amounted to $296 per person. On July 1, 1962, the liquidation of the reservation was over. As far as the federal government was concerned, the Catawba Indians, like the New Reservation, ceased to exist.

Many others took the government's view, and once again predictions of the death of the Catawba Nation were common. "A Nation Dies Slowly," proclaimed the headline in a Charleston newspaper in 1962; "Catawba Nation Dying," announced another. There was plenty of evidence to support this view. After 1962 the Indians had no formal government, and in 1966 the Catawba school recessed for the last time. Even before then many Indians had sold their lands, as the opponents of termination had predicted they would. Without land, the dispersal of the people accelerated as they moved to nearby towns

In the tradition of his forebears, Chief Gilbert Blue, photographed in 1985, continues to represent his people to the non-Indian community.

in search of jobs or education. In the wider world they were treated as whites: They lived in white neighborhoods, worked in white factories, and went to hotels, restaurants, movie theaters, and public restrooms that, be-

cause of segregation laws, were legally restricted to whites. The prediction of *The Book of Mormon* seemed to be coming true.

And yet today it appears that Catawbas are once again defying outsiders' predictions. Three factors explain their remarkable persistence. First, the Old Reservation, those 630 acres still held for the tribe by the state as they have been since the 1840s, gives Catawbas a home to which they can always return. Second, the Mormon church remains, as it has for a century, a spiritual and social anchor providing the Indians with a distinct identity. Finally, Catawba pottery, still produced by some of the older women, gives the people a physical link with their Indian heritage.

Building on these foundations, the Catawba Nation has undergone a rebirth since the early 1970s. In 1973, Catawbas reestablished the office of chief and elected Samuel Blue's grandson, Gilbert Blue, to the position. In 1974, Indians began drifting back to the Old Reservation, setting up mobile homes on vacant land and putting down roots in their ancestral soil. Pottery classes were started so that Catawba elders could pass this ancient skill on to the next generation. There was also talk of beginning language classes based on the stories collected by Frank Speck so that Catawbas could once again speak the words of their ancestors, words that had been unheard for so long.

Since the 1970s, the most obvious example of the Nation's new lease on life has been its campaign to reclaim the lands it lost in the treaty of 1840. The Indians argue that the treaty is invalid because it was never ratified by the U.S. Congress, as a federal law of 1790 required of all treaties with Indians. Thus the reservation originally granted to Catawbas by the king of England in 1763—all 144,000 acres of it—should still belong to the Nation. This land, now home to more than 50,000 people, both Catawbas and non-Indians, is worth an estimated $2 billion. At no point have the Catawbas demanded all of this land back; rather, they have pushed for a settlement of their claims that would provide the Indians with a new and larger reservation along with money for tribal development through business, education, and community activities.

After exhaustive discussions with local, state, and federal authorities in the 1970s failed to reach a settlement, the Indians took their case to court. The suit first went to federal district court in October 1980. The Catawbas were seeking $1 billion in reparations for the loss of their land and 140 years of back rent and damages. In June 1982 the district court judge dismissed all of the Indians' claims on the grounds that they were no longer effective under the statute of limitations imposed when the Catawbas accepted termination in 1959. Moreover, the judge ruled that the Indians' approval of termination had essentially destroyed the Catawbas as a tribe. The Catawbas then appealed to the 4th Circuit Court of Appeals in Richmond, Virginia. In October 1983 a three-member panel of judges decided in favor of the Indians. They ruled that the Catawbas' acceptance of termination and the statute of limitations imposed by it applied only to their relationship with the federal government and had no bearing on the Catawbas' older claim against the state of South Carolina. The case then went to the U.S. Supreme Court, which ruled in June 1986 that the statute of limitations did apply to the suit. The justices did not, however, rule on the validity of the claim itself, and sent the case back to the 4th Circuit Court of Appeals to determine if the suit was indeed valid. Nearly a decade after the suit was first brought, it still awaited a final decision. "We haven't given up," Chief Gilbert Blue said in 1986 of the Supreme Court decision.

The efforts by Gilbert Blue and his people to reclaim their homeland are characteristic of Catawba history. Like Hagler and others before him, Catawbas today are still balancing past and present, combining devotion to ancestors and friendship with whites. In trying to regain some of their ancient territory, they are trying to recapture part of their past. Yet they have been more ready to talk than to fight, and when they had to, to fight using a system of laws that had its origin in another cultural tradition. Whether or not they win this particular battle, it seems clear that the Catawbas' struggle to blend old and new will go on, flowing into the future like the river that bears their name. ▲

BIBLIOGRAPHY

Blumer, Thomas J., comp. *Bibliography of the Catawba.* Metuchen, NJ: Scarecrow Press, 1987.

Brown, Douglas Summers. *The Catawba Indians: The People of the River.* Columbia: University of South Carolina Press, 1966.

Hudson, Charles M. *The Catawba Nation.* University of Georgia Monographs, no. 18. Athens: University of Georgia Press, 1970.

Lawson, John. *A New Voyage to Carolina.* Edited by Hugh T. Lefler. Chapel Hill: University of North Carolina Press, 1967.

Merrell, James H. *The Indians' New World: Catawbas and their Neighbors, 1540–1850.* Chapel Hill: University of North Carolina Press, 1989.

Mooney, James. *The Siouan Tribes of the East.* Smithsonian Institution, Bureau of American Ethnology, bulletin no. 22. Washington, D.C.: Government Printing Office, 1894.

Scaife, H. Lewis. *History and Condition of the Catawba Indians of South Carolina.* Philadelphia: Office of the Indian Rights Association, 1896.

Speck, Frank G. *Catawba Texts.* Columbia University Contributions to Anthropology, vol. 24. New York: Columbia University Press, 1934.

THE CATAWBAS AT A GLANCE

TRIBE *Catawbas*

CULTURE AREA *Southern Piedmont*

GEOGRAPHY *Carolina Piedmont*

LINGUISTIC FAMILY *Eastern Siouan*

TRADITIONAL ECONOMY *agriculture, hunting, gathering*

FIRST CONTACT *Hernando de Soto, Spanish, 1540*

CURRENT POPULATION *1,300*

FEDERAL STATUS *nonrecognized*

GLOSSARY

acculturation The process by which one culture changes and adapts to the dominant culture it confronts.

agent; Indian agent A person appointed by the Bureau of Indian Affairs to supervise U.S. government programs on a reservation and/or in a specific region; after 1908 the title "superintendent" replaced "agent."

archaeology The recovery and study of evidence of human ways of life, especially that of prehistoric peoples.

Archaic period The period from about 10,000 to 3,000 B.P. when people in North America began using stone and bone tools and obtained food by hunting and gathering. It was generally characterized by seasonal migrations and the use of fire and showed effective use of local natural resources.

band A territorially based, simply organized group of people who are economically dependent on hunting and gathering.

Bureau of Indian Affairs (BIA) A U.S. government agency established in 1824 and assigned to the Department of the Interior in 1849. Originally intended to manage trade and other relations with Indians, the BIA now seeks to develop and implement programs to encourage Indians to manage their own affairs and to improve their educational opportunities and general social and economic well-being.

culture The learned behavior of humans; nonbiological, socially taught activities; the way of life of a group of people.

eractasswa A Catawba word meaning *chief.*

Esaws The English rendering of *yeh iswah h'reh,* the Catawbas' name for themselves.

headmen Leaders of a tribe, also called councillors because they served as the tribe's council. Among the Catawbas, these men were usually chosen from the heads of each family.

horticulture Food production using human muscle power and simple hand tools to plant and harvest domesticated crops.

hunting-and-gathering; foraging An economic system of hunting wild animals, fishing, and gathering wild plant foods; the most ancient way for humans to obtain the necessities of life.

Indian Reorganization Act The 1934 federal law that ended the policy of allotting plots of land to individuals and provided for political and economic development of reservation communities.

Mississippian culture A way of life that flourished in many parts of the Southeast from A.D. 700 to 1500. Mississippian cultures were characterized by social classes; the people built temple mounds and engaged in trade over a wide area.

nation An Indian group comprising several tribes.

Paleo-Indian period The period in North America lasting until about 10,000 years ago, when human culture involved hunting large mammals and making specialized stone tools.

Piedmont The hilly region lying between the Atlantic coastal plain and the Appalachian Mountains and extending from southern New York to Georgia.

Pleistocene A geologic period ending in North America before 10,000 years ago, marked by the advance and retreat of glaciers.

projectile points Stone weapon tips that were attached to wooden shafts to form spears or lances.

religious healer A spiritual leader and curer who used his special knowledge of natural remedies and access to the spirit world to cure ailments and solve problems.

removal policy National policy, begun in 1830, calling for the sale of all Indian land in the eastern and southern United States and the migration of Indians from these areas to lands across the Mississippi River.

reservation A tract of land set aside by treaty for Indian occupation and use.

segregation A system of laws adopted by southern states in the late 19th century to separate the races in most areas of daily life. The policy lasted in many places until the 1960s.

Siouan The family of languages spoken by Catawbas and other Indians of the Piedmont, as well as by the Sioux tribes of the Great Plains.

sweathouse or **sweat lodge** An airtight hut in which rituals are held while steam is produced by pouring water over heated rocks. Sweathouse ceremonies are conducted to achieve a condition of spiritual purification.

treaty A contract negotiated between representatives of the United States or another national government and one or more Indian tribes. Treaties dealt with surrender of political independence, peaceful relations, land sales, boundaries, and related matters.

tribe A society consisting of several or many separate communities united by kinship, common culture, language, and such social units as clans, religious organizations, and economic and political institutions. Tribes are generally characterized by economic and political equality and thus lack social classes and authoritative chiefs.

Woodland period The time when people in North America practiced horticulture, made pottery, used the bow and arrow, buried their dead in cemeteries marked by mounds of earth, and lived in permanent villages. The Eastern Woodland period lasted from about 10,000 to 3,000 years ago.

workings A term used among the Catawbas to mean voluntary labor on behalf of a neighbor in need.

yeh iswah h'reh The name Catawbas used for themselves, meaning "people of the river."

INDEX

PICTURE CREDITS

JAMES H. MERRELL is assistant professor of history at Vassar College. He holds B.A. degrees from Lawrence University and from Oxford University and received his M.A. and Ph.D. from Johns Hopkins University. He has been a fellow at both the D'Arcy McNickle Center for the History of the American Indian at the Newberry Library in Chicago and the Institute of Early American History and Culture in Williamsburg, Virginia. Combining his interests in American Indians and colonial American history, he has written several articles on relations between Indians and colonists in eastern North America. In addition, he is coeditor of *Beyond the Covenant Chain: The Iroquois and Their Neighbors in Indian North America, 1600–1800* and author of *The Indians' New World: Catawbas and their Neighbors from European Contact through the Removal Era.*

FRANK W. PORTER III, general editor of INDIANS OF NORTH AMERICA, is director of the Chelsea House Foundation for American Indian Studies. He holds a B.A., M.A., and Ph.D. from the University of Maryland. He has done extensive research concerning the Indians of Maryland and Delaware and is the author of numerous articles on their history, archaeology, geography, and ethnography. He was formerly director of the Maryland Commission on Indian Affairs and American Indian Research and Resource Institute, Gettysburg, Pennsylvania, and he has received grants from the Delaware Humanities Forum, the Maryland Committee for the Humanities, the Ford Foundation, and the National Endowment for the Humanities, among others. Dr. Porter is the author of *The Bureau of Indian Affairs* in the Chelsea House KNOW YOUR GOVERNMENT series.

DATE			

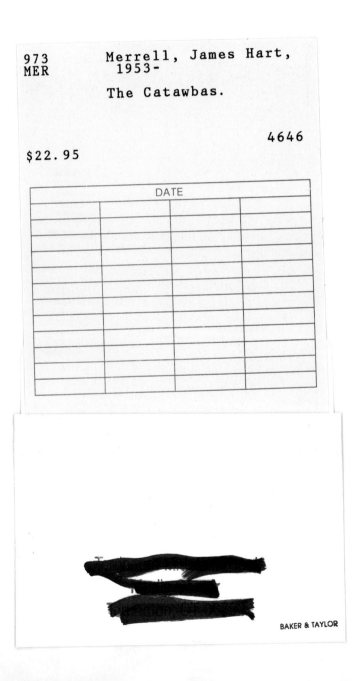